THE FEMININE
MYSTIC

THE FEMININE
MYSTIC

readings from
early spiritual writers

Edited by
LYNNE M. DEMING

THE PILGRIM PRESS
CLEVELAND, OHIO

The Pilgrim Press, Cleveland, Ohio 44115

© 1997 by The Pilgrim Press

Pages 160–162 constitute an extension of this copyright page.

All rights reserved. Published 1997

Printed in the United States of America on acid-free paper

02 01 00 99 98 97   5 4 3 2 1

Library of Congress Cataloging-in Publication Data

The feminine mystic : readings from early spiritual writers
    / edited by Lynne M. Deming.
        p.   cm.
    Includes bibliographical references.
    ISBN 0-8298-1167-2 (pbk. : alk. paper)
    1. Spiritual life—Christianity.   2. Mysticism.
3. Women mystics.
BV4501.2.F44   1997
248—DC21   97-12040
                                                    CIP
                                                    Rev.

CONTENTS

Introduction

You who would read this book,
If you indeed wish to grasp it,
Think about what you say,
For it is very difficult to comprehend.
                                    —*Marguerite Porete*

The Feminine Mystic collects the writings of thirteen women mystics and organizes these writings according to themes. The women who contributed to this book lived in tumultuous times spanning several centuries, from 1098 to 1633. They were from England, the Rhineland, France, Italy, and the Lowlands. Their backgrounds varied from noble birth to working class. Some were well-educated; others taught themselves. Yet the common thread that runs through their lives is their deep and passionate love for God and the compulsion to express that relationship in writing.

The categories into which the writings are organized range from emotions such as fear and love to issues of the day such as justice and authority to theological themes such as grace and faith to spiritual disciplines such as prayer and discernment. We are grateful to these women for the legacy of wisdom they have left us.

This book grew out of the work we do annually on *In Good Company: A Woman's Journal for Spiritual Reflection.* That journal provides one quote for each day of the year and space for reflection in response to those quotes. In compiling *In Good Company* we use various sources, including the writings of women mystics. So we decided to explore the idea of doing a book on the women mystics, and began reading the various collections of writings that are now available.

In our research we discovered many volumes devoted to the writings of women mystics, but the corpus of literature is largely organized by the writings of a single mystic within a single volume. We began to ask ourselves whether it would also be interesting to organize these writings around themes that were relevant to the mystics themselves and also to us today. And so this book began to take shape in our minds.

On a warm day in the summer of 1996, a group of women gathered and began to read through the literature we had collected. We were looking for themes, for common threads that emerged as we skimmed through the material. Although we had created a list of themes beforehand, the project took on a life of its own as these women began to speak to us. When the day was over we had accumulated a variety of themes and selections, and what remained was to organize those into a volume that would have integrity and be interesting to our readers.

As we worked through that phase of the editorial process, we made several decisions along the way. First, rather than using our original list of themes, we allowed the themes to choose themselves as we read through the material, resulting in an unevenness in the length of individual selections and the number of selections for each theme. Our original intention was to provide a week's worth of readings for each theme. Since we could not fit the readings we selected into that pattern, we allowed the book to create itself instead. The resulting volume is more spontaneous and better reflects the nature of the material itself. After all, these mystics wrote from their hearts and not from a predetermined list of topics.

Second, we made a decision along the way about the use of language in these readings. Our original idea was to edit all this material for inclusive language. But the longer we worked with the material the more problematic that approach became. Thorough inclusive language editing would have produced readings much different from the original writing and would have required extensive permissions work with the copyright holders of the material. If we had used brackets to indicate our changes, they would have interfered with the readings. So we chose to leave the language as it was in the original, hoping that our selections show a richness in the variety of theological images included.

Finally, as we were worked with the selections the need for biographical information became clear. Thanks to K.C. Ackley for writing the resulting biographies that appear at the back of the book.

We can imagine a number of ways in which this book can be used. If you are interested in a particular topic, you can read the selection(s) for that topic in one sitting. We have alphabetized these topics so that they will be easy to find. Or, you can read straight through the volume—either as an intellectual exercise or as food for thought as you write in a journal. We can also imagine a women's study group using this book as a resource. The readings should produce some lively discussions among women who are interested in the theology and life issues faced by the women in the book. However you choose to use this book, we hope you find these selections to be fascinating reading.

> *Humble, then, your wisdom*
> *Which is based on Reason,*
> *And place all your fidelity*
> *In those things which are given*
> *By Love, illuminated through Faith.*
> *And thus you will understand this book*
> *Which makes the Soul live by love.*
>
> *—Marguerite Porete*

Many thanks to the group of women who put this volume together: K.C. Ackley, Leah Matthews, Audrey Miller, and Marj Pon. The experience was one of those rare moments when work merges with fun. Thanks also to Marj for designing the text, to Mary Tuttle for keying in the manuscript, and to Martha Clark for commissioning Katie Burdett's art and for designing the cover.

LYNNE MOBBERLEY DEMING

THE FEMININE
MYSTIC

ABANDONMENT

CATHERINE OF GENOA

You are endangering me to excess.
I feel the roots that attach me to life cut,
and find myself quite abandoned.
All you do is concentrate on heaven and forget me.
It seems to me that you seek to undo me with
    fiery arrows
that pierce me to the quick.
You make me cry out in pain,
and would have me go scurrying about madly on
    all fours.

Her humanity cried out with a loud voice and no one paid heed. Those present concurred that no greater suffering was ever witnessed in a body to all appearances healthy. Seeing her immersed in such pain, those who were ministering to her and those devoted to her hoped for a speedy death.

Serge Hughes, trans., *Catherine of Genoa: Purgation and Purgatory, The Spiritual Dialogue,* The Classics of Western Spirituality (New York: Paulist Press, 1979), 140.

ABANDONMENT

MECHTHILD OF MAGDEBURG

You must love no-thingness,
You must flee something,
You must remain alone
And go to nobody.
You must be very active
And free of all things.
You must deliver the captives

And force those who are free.
You must comfort the sick
And yet have nothing yourself.
You must drink the water of suffering
And light the fire of Love with the wood
of the virtues.
Thus you live in the true desert.

Emilie Zum Brunn and Georgette Epiney-Burgard, *Women Mystics in Medieval Europe* (New York: Paragon House, 1989), 60.

ABANDONMENT

TERESA OF AVILA

The diligence on our part that comes to my mind as being the most effective is the following. First, we must always ask God in prayer to sustain us, and very often think that if He abandons us we will soon end in the abyss, as is true; and we must never trust in ourselves since it would be foolish to do so. Then, we should walk with special care and attention, observing how we are proceeding in the practice of virtue: whether we are getting better or worse in some area, especially in love for one another, in the desire to be considered the least among the Sisters, and in the performance of ordinary tasks. For if we look out for these things and ask the Lord to enlighten us, we will soon see the gain or the loss. Don't think that a soul that comes so close to God is allowed to lose Him so quickly, that the devil has an easy task. His Majesty would regret the loss of this soul so much that He gives it in many ways a thousand interior warnings, so that the harm will not be hidden from it.

Kieran Kavanaugh and Otilio Rodriguez, trans., *Teresa of Avila: The Interior Castle,* The Classics of Western Spirituality (New York: Paulist Press, 1979), 106.

ATONEMENT

CATHERINE OF SIENA

[God says:] Atonement is made, then, through the desire of the soul who is united to me, infinite Good, in proportion as love is perfect both in the one who prays with desire and in the one who receives. And my goodness will measure out to you with the very same measure that you give to me and that the other receives. So feed the flame of your desire and let not a moment pass without crying out for these others in my presence with humble voice and constant prayer. Thus I tell you and the spiritual father I have given you on earth: Behave courageously, and die to all your selfish sensuality!

Suzanne Noffke, trans., *Catherine of Siena: The Dialogue,* The Classics of Western Spirituality (New York: Paulist Press, 1980), 32–33.

AUTHORITY

CATHERINE OF SIENA

[God says:] No rank, whether civil or divine law, can be held in grace without holy justice. For those who are not corrected and those who do not correct are like members beginning to rot, and if the doctor were only to apply ointment without cauterizing the wound, the whole body would become fetid and corrupt.

So it is with prelates or with anyone else in authority. If they see the members who are their subjects rotting because of the filth of deadly sin and apply only the ointment of soft words without reproof, they will never get well. Rather, they will infect the other members with whom they form one body under their one shepherd. But if those in authority are truly good doctors to those souls, as were those glorious shepherds, they will not use ointment with-

4

 out the fire of reproof. And if the members are still obstinate in their evildoing, they will cut them off from the congregation so that they will not infect the whole body with the filth of deadly sin.

But [those who are in authority] today do not do this. In fact, they pretend not to see. And do you know why? Because the root of selfish love is alive in them, and this is the source of their perverse slavish fear. They do not correct people for fear of losing their rank and position and their material possessions. They act as if they were blind, so they do not know how to maintain their positions. For if they saw how it is by holy justice that their positions are to be maintained, they would maintain them. But because they are bereft of light they do not know this. They believe they can succeed through injustice, by not reproving the sins of their subjects. But they are deceived by their own sensual passion, by their hankering for civil or ecclesiastical rank.

Another reason they will not correct others is that they themselves are living in the same or greater sins. They sense that the same guilt envelops them, so they cast aside fervor and confidence and, chained by slavish fear, pretend they do not see. Even what they do see they do not correct, but let themselves be won over by flattery and bribes, using these very things as excuses for not punishing the offenders. In them is fulfilled what my Truth said in the holy Gospel:"They are blind and leaders of the blind. And if one blind person leads another, they both fall into the ditch."

Suzanne Noffke, trans., *Catherine of Siena: The Dial0ogue,* The Classics of Western Spirituality (New York: Paulist Press, 1980), 224-225.

AWAKENING

MARGARET EBNER

Often from his goodness God gives me an invitation saying, "Get up, I want to give you special graces today," or sometimes, "Get up, I want to give you what no eye has seen nor ear has heard and what has never yet come to a human heart. That was all granted to me lovingly with the sweet Name Jesus Christus. But what has drawn me away from delight in eating and drinking is the great delight and sweetness that I feel from God and which I await from Him in Christian love— to enjoy Him eternally in His divine clarity.

Leonard Hindsley, trans. and ed., *Margaret Ebner: Major Works,* The Classics of Western Spirituality (Mahwah, N.J.: Paulist Press, 1993), 127.

CHARITY

HILDEGARD OF BINGEN

Love or charity also brought the Only-Begotten Word of God from the bosom of God in heaven and placed the Word in the womb of a mother on earth. She scorned neither sinners nor publicans, but instead strained in childbirth in order that all people might be saved. She also softened the fountain of tears falling from the eyes of the faithful, often leading away the hardness of their hearts. Humility and charity are clearly virtues; they are like a soul and body; strong people have the forces of a soul and the members of a body. What does this mean? Humility is like a soul and charity is like a body; they cannot be separated by some internal change, but they work together. Similarly, neither the soul nor the body would be strong if they were separated from each other, but they work together as long as a person lives in a body. And just as various powers of the various members of the body have been subjugated to the soul and to the body, so also the other virtues in accordance with justice work for humility and charity. Therefore, o people, follow humility and charity for the glory of God and for your salvation. Armed with humility and charity, you do not need to fear the snares of the devil, but you will possess everlasting life.

Bruce Hozeski, trans., *Hildegard von Bingen's Mystical Visions: Translated from Scivias,* introduced by Matthew Fox (Santa Fe: Bear & Company, 1995), 236–37.

CHARITY

MARGUERITE PORETE

Charity obeys no created thing except Love.

Charity possesses nothing of her own, and should she possess something she does not say that it belongs to her.

Charity abandons her own need and attends to that of others.

Charity asks no payment from any creature for some good or pleasure that she has accomplished.

Charity has no shame, nor fear, nor anxiety. She is so upright that she cannot bow on account of anything that might happen to her.

Charity neither makes nor takes account of anything under the sun, for the whole world is only refuse and leftovers.

Charity gives to all what she possesses of worth, without retaining anything for herself, and with this she often promises what she does not possess through her great largesse, in the hope that the more she gives the more remains in her.

Charity is such a wise merchant that she earns profits everywhere where others lose, and she escapes the bonds that bind others and thus she has great multiplicity of what pleases Love.

Ellen L. Babinsky, trans., *Marguerite Porete: The Mirror of Simple Souls,* The Classics of Western Spirituality (Mahwah, N.J.: Paulist Press, 1993), 82.

CHOOSING GOOD/CHOOSING GOD

ANGELA OF FOLIGNO

Discovering that God is good, the soul loves him for his goodness. Loving him, it desires to possess him, it gives all that it has and can have, even its own self, in order to possess him; and in possessing him, the soul experiences and tastes his sweetness. Possessing, experiencing, tasting God himself, the supreme and infinite sweetness, it enjoys him with the greatest delight.

Then, enamored with the sweetness of the Beloved, the soul desires to hold him; desiring to hold him, it embraces him; embracing him, it binds and weds itself to God, and finds God bound and wedded to itself in the sweetest form of love. Then the power of love transforms the lover into the Beloved and the Beloved into the lover. This means that, set ablaze by divine love, the soul is transformed by the power of love into God the Beloved whom it loves with such sweetness. Just as hot iron put into the fire takes on the form of fire—its heat, color, power, force—and almost becomes fire itself, as it gives itself completely and not partially while retaining its own substance, similarly, the soul, united to God and with God by the perfect fire of divine love, gives itself, as it were, totally and throws itself into God. Transformed into God, without having lost its own substance, its entire life is changed and through this love it becomes almost totally divine.

For this transformation to happen, it is necessary that knowledge come first, and the love follows which transforms the lover into the Beloved. This is how the soul which knows God in truth and loves him with fervor is transformed into the Good it knows and loves with such fervor.

Ellen L. Babinsky, trans., *Marguerite Porete: The Mirror of Simple Souls*, The Classics of Western Spirituality (Mahwah, N.J.: Paulist Press, 1993), 82.

CHOOSING GOOD/CHOOSING GOD

HILDEGARD OF BINGEN

Knowledge exists in humans as if it were in a mirror, for the desire to will good or evil is concealed within them. When a person is placed between two choices, the person bends himself or herself toward the choice he or she desires. But the person who bends toward the good and embraces that faithful work with the help of God will receive the pay of blessed remuneration because he or she scorned evil and did the good. The person who bends toward the evil and swallows this perverse action through the suggestion of the devil will run into the punishments of just retribution because he or she neglected the good and continued with the evil. Therefore, a person who submits himself or herself to God with devotion and humility may work out his or her own salvation. This salvation flows from the highest good. So his or her soul is saturated with innermost holiness, because the person served the creator with a good disposition and out of fear of God, as it should be.

Bruce Hozeski, trans., *Hildegard von Bingen's Mystical Visions: Translated from Scivias,* introduced by Matthew Fox (Santa Fe: Bear & Company, 1995), 236-37.

CHOOSING GOOD/CHOOSING GOD

JULIAN OF NORWICH

O God, out of your goodness, give me yourself, for you are enough for me. I can ask nothing less that would be fully to your glory. And if I do ask anything less, I will always be in need, since it is only in you that I have all!

Our Lord often said to me: "I am It! I am the One! I am what is highest! I am what you love! I am what delights you! I am what you serve! I am what you long for! I am what you want! I am what you intend! I am everything that is! I am what the Holy Church preaches and teaches you! I am the One who showed myself to you here!"

José De Vinck, *Revelations of Women Mystics: From Middle Ages to Modern Times* (New York: Alba House, 1985), 72-73.

CHOOSING GOOD/CHOOSING GOD

JULIAN OF NORWICH

And thus I understood that any man or woman who deliberately chooses God in this life, out of love, may be sure that he or she is loved without end. This endless love produces grace in them. For God wants us to hold trustfully to this: that we be as certain, in hope, of the bliss of heaven while we are here as we will be, in fact, when we are there. And always the more delight and joy we take in this certainty, with reverence and meekness, the better it pleases him.

Some of us believe God is almighty and may do everything, and that he is all-wise and can do everything—but that he is all love and shall do all, that we fail to see.

José De Vinck, *Revelations of Women Mystics: From Middle Ages to Modern Times* (New York: Alba House, 1985), 74.

COMFORT

JULIAN OF NORWICH

This vision was shown to my intellect to teach me that it is good for some souls to have such an experience—alternations of comfort with distress and abandonment. God wants us to know that he is safeguarding us, as much in woe as in happiness. For the good of his soul, a man is sometimes left to himself, without sin being the cause of it—since at the time I had committed no sin that would have caused me to be left to myself: it happened unexpectedly. Nor did I deserve to enjoy the feeling of blessedness: our Lord gave it to me freely, as he pleased. And sometimes he allows us to suffer misery—but both are one and the same love.

José De Vinck, *Revelations of Women Mystics: From Middle Ages to Modern Times* (New York: Alba House, 1985), 63.

COMMITMENT

CATHERINE OF GENOA

Since I am subject to you, I will do as you wish;
remember, though, that without me you cannot
  do what you wish.
let us, therefore, understand each other at the
  outset;
in this way we shall have no arguments.
Once I have found what gives me joy, please
  keep your word.
I would not want to hear you grumble,
muttering that you want to go elsewhere
or insisting on looking for what interests you.
To do away with that possibility,
let us invite a third party to come along,
someone to resolve any differences we might have
—a just and unselfish person.

Serge Hughes, trans., *Catherine of Genoa: Purgation and Purgatory, The Spiritual Dialogue,* The Classics of Western Spirituality (New York: Paulist Press, 1979), 91.

DISCERNMENT

CATHERINE OF SIENA

[God says:] Charity, it is true, has many offshoots, like a tree with many branches. But what gives life to both the tree and its branches is its root, so long as that root is planted in the soil of humility. For humility is the governess and wet nurse of the charity into which this branch of discernment is engrafted. Now the source of humility, as I have already told you, is the soul's true knowledge of herself and of my goodness. So only when discernment is rooted in humility is it virtuous, producing life-giving fruit and willingly yielding what is due to everyone.

In the first place, the soul gives glory and praise to my name for the graces and gifts she knows she has received from me. And to herself she gives what she sees herself deserving of. She knows that all that she is and every gift she has is from me, not from herself, and to me she attributes all. In fact, she considers herself worthy of punishment for her ingratitude in the face of so many favors, and negligent in her use of the time and graces I have given her. So she repays herself with contempt and regret for her sins. Such is the work of the virtue of discernment, rooted in self-knowledge and true humility.

Without this humility, as I have said, the soul would be without discernment. For lack of discernment is set in pride, just as discernment is set in humility. A soul without discernment would, like a thief, rob me of my honor and bestow it on herself for her own glory. And what was her own doing she would blame on me, grumbling and complaining about my mysterious ways with her and with the rest of my creatures, constantly finding cause for scandal in me and in her neighbors.

Not so those who have the virtue of discernment. These give what is due to me and to themselves. And then they give their neighbors what is due them: first of all, loving charity and constant humble prayer—your mutual debt—and the debt of teaching, and the example of a holy and honorable life, and the counsel and help they need for their salvation.

If you have this virtue, then whatever your state in life may be—whether noble or superior or subject—all that you do for your neighbors will be done with discernment and loving charity. For discernment and charity are engrafted together and planted in the soil of that true humility which is born of self-knowledge.

Suzanne Noffke, trans., *Catherine of Siena: The Dialogue,* The Classics of Western Spirituality (New York: Paulist Press, 1980), 40–41.

DISCERNMENT

CATHERINE OF SIENA

[God says:] Imagine a circle traced on the ground, and in its center a tree sprouting with a shoot grafted into its side. The tree finds its nourishment in the soil within the expanse of the circle, but uprooted from the soil it would die fruitless. So think of the soul as a tree made for love and living only by love. Indeed, without this divine love, which is true and perfect charity, death would be her fruit instead of life. The circle in which this tree's root, the soul's love, must grow is true knowledge of herself, knowledge that is joined to me, who like the circle have neither beginning nor end. You can go round and round within this circle, finding neither end nor beginning, yet never leaving the circle. This knowledge of yourself, and of me within yourself, is grounded in the soil of true humility, which is as great as the expanse of the circle (which is the knowledge of yourself united with me, as I have said). But if your knowledge of yourself were isolated from me there would be no full circle at all. Instead, there would be a beginning in self-knowledge, but apart from me it would end in confusion.

So the tree of charity is nurtured in humility and branches out in true discernment. The marrow of the tree (that is, loving charity within the soul) is patience, a sure sign that I am in her and that she is united with me.

This tree, so delightfully planted, bears many-fragranced blossoms of virtue. Its fruit is grace for the soul herself and blessing for her neighbors in proportion to the conscientiousness of those who would share my servants' fruits. To me this tree yields the fragrance of glory and praise to my name, and so it does what I created it for and comes at last to its goal, to me, everlasting Life, life that cannot be taken from you against your will.

And every fruit produced by this tree is seasoned with discernment, and this unites them all, as I have told you.

Suzanne Noffke, trans., *Catherine of Siena: The Dialogue,* The Classics of Western Spirituality (New York: Paulist Press, 1980), 41-42.

DISCERNMENT

HADEWIJCH OF ANTWERP (BRABANT)

And nearby stood a tree with many branches; it was tall and extended all its branches through those of another tree. And the Angel said to me again:"O wise one, instructed by reason, even by the reason of the great God, read and understand the wise and longsighted lesson that teaches those who grow up through one another!"And I understood that it could be read on each leaf:"I am discernment: without me you can do nothing" (John 15:5).

Mother Columba Hart, trans., *Hadewijch: The Complete Works,* The Classics of Western Spirituality (New York: Paulist Press, 1980), 264.

FAITH

CATHERINE OF SIENA

[God says:] How do they have this pledge in life? Let me tell you:They see my goodness in themselves and they know my truth when their understanding—which is the soul's eye—is enlightened in me.The pupil of the eye is most holy faith, and this light of faith enables them to discern and know and follow the way and teaching of my Truth, the incarnate Word.Without this pupil, which is faith, they would see no more than a person who has eyes, but with a film covering the pupils that give the eyes sight. It is the same with the eye of understanding. Its pupil is faith, but if selfish love pulls over it the film of infidelity, it cannot see. It may have the appearance of an eye, but it is sightless because infidelity has deprived it of light. So seeing me these souls know me, and knowing me they love me.And in loving me their selfish will is swallowed up and lost.

Having lost their own selfish will they clothe themselves in mine. But I will nothing less than your holiness. So at once they set about turning their backs on the way beneath the bridge and begin to mount the bridge.They cross through the thorns without being hurt, because their feet (that is, their affections) are shod with my will. This is why I told you that they suffer physically but not spiritually, because their sensual will—which afflicts and pains the spirit—is dead. Since they bear everything with reverence, considering it a grace to suffer for me. And they want nothing but what I will.

If I send them suffering at the hand of the demons, allowing them to be much tempted in order to test their virtue, they stand firm. For they have strengthened their will in me by humbling themselves, considering themselves unworthy of spiritual peace and quiet and deserving of suffering. For this reason they pass through life joyfully, knowing themselves and untroubled by suffering. . . .

It is indeed the truth then that these souls have a foretaste and guarantee of eternal life even in this life. They do not lose their lives in the water; when they pass through the thorns they are not pricked, because they have known me, Good itself, and they have sought that goodness where it is to be found, in the Word, my only-begotten Son.

Suzanne Noffke, trans., *Catherine of Siena: The Dialogue*, The Classics of Western Spirituality (New York: Paulist Press, 1980), 92-94.

FAITH

MARGARET EBNER

I had strong faith and powerful trust in God; yet, even so, I had a human fear of death. I was no longer sure that I would live and I awaited only the mercy of God to receive my soul. As I lay there I felt inner sweet, divine grace spreading outward through my body. I could feel myself again and came to myself once more with divine grace. Meanwhile the faithful Friend of our Lord and my entire convent had been in great sorrow because of me. They now rejoiced all the more because they had taken great pains for me before God by singing and reading. That Friday I awoke again with great pain and suffering, which was taken away from me again by great divine joy. It was revealed to me forcefully that our Lord wanted to accomplish in all His friends the words that He spoke to His disciples, "Your sorrow will be changed into joy, etc." . . . At the same time the Name *Jesus Christ* us was so forcefully impressed upon me that since that time only prayers in which the Name of Jesus Christ came forth and those concerned with our Lord's works of love were consoling and appealing to me.

Leonard Hindsley, trans. and ed., *Margaret Ebner: Major Works,* The Classics of Western Spirituality (Mahwah, N.J.: Paulist Press, 1993), 101–2.

FEAR

CATHERINE OF SIENA

[God says:] Then comes the wind of slavish fear, which makes them afraid of their own shadow, afraid to lose what they love. Or they fear the loss of their own lives or their children's or someone else's. Or they are afraid they will lose their position, or others will lose theirs—and all this because of their selfish love for themselves or for honor or wealth. Such fear lets them enjoy nothing in peace. They do not hold what they have with respect for my priorities, and so they are dogged by slavish, cringing fear, made the wretched slaves of sin. Now one can consider oneself as good as what one serves. And sin is a nothing, so these souls have become nothings.

While the wind of fear is battering them the wind of trouble and adversity (the very thing they feared) joins in and takes away their possessions, sometimes this thing or that, sometimes life itself, when the power of death deprives them of everything. Sometimes, though, it takes only now one thing, now another: health, children, riches, position, honors—whatever I the gentle doctor see to be necessary for their salvation and so allow it to happen. But if their weakness has turned to rottenness and they are wholly lacking in discernment, the fruit of patience spoils. Then impatience sprouts, along with outrage and complaining and hatred and contempt for me and everyone else, and what I have given for life becomes death to the receivers, with grief in proportion to their selfishness.

Suzanne Noffke, trans., *Catherine of Siena: The Dialogue,* The Classics of Western Spirituality (New York: Paulist Press, 1980), 174–75.

FEAR

HILDEGARD OF BINGEN

Dread, which is the beginning of anxiousness, causes fear. Fear, however, agitates trembling which ought to cause a person to be just. Why is this? A person begins to be anxious when he or she dreads somethings. This is caused by the power of reason which is a gift of the Holy Spirit. And with the power of reason, a person knows God. With the knowledge which the person has of God, the person begins to fear because he or she fears those things which are of God with zeal, then the fiery grace of Christ will shake the person, and this makes the person tremble. A person is terrified as he or she performs the justice of God.

Bruce Hozeski, trans., *Hildegard von Bingen's Mystical Visions: Translated from Scivias,* introduced by Matthew Fox (Santa Fe: Bear & Company, 1995), 237.

FEAR

JULIAN OF NORWICH

For I saw four kinds of fear. One fear of assault, which comes to a man suddenly through timidity. This fear is good, for it helps to purge a man, as does bodily sickness or such other pains which are not sinful; for all such pains help one if they are patiently accepted. The second is fear of pain, through which a man is stirred and wakened from the sleep of sin; for anyone fast asleep in sin is not for that time able to receive the gentle strength of the Holy Spirit, until he has obtained this fear of pain and of the fire of purgatory. And this fear moves him to seek comfort and mercy of God; and so this fear helps him as though by chance, and enables him to have contrition by the blessed teaching of the Holy Spirit. The third is a doubtful fear; if it be recognized for what it is, however little it may be, it is a kind of despair. For I am certain that God hates all doubtful fear, and he wishes us to drive it out, knowing truly how we may live. The fourth is reverent fear, for there is no fear in us which pleases him but reverent fear, and that is very sweet and gentle, because our love is great. And yet this reverent fear is not the same as love; they are different in kind and in effect, and neither of them may be obtained without the other.

Therefore I am sure that he who loves, he fears, though he may feel little of this. Whatever kinds of fear be suggested to us other than reverent fear, though they appear disguised as holiness, they are not so true; and this is how they can be recognized and distinguished, one from the other. The more that one has of this reverent fear, the more it softens and strengthens and pleases and gives rest; and false fear belabours and assails and perturbs. So that the remedy is to recognize them both and to reject false fear, just as we should an evil spirit who presented himself in the likeness of a good angel. For it is so with an evil spirit; though he may come under the disguise and likeness of a good angel, with his dalliance and his operations, however fair he may appear, he first belabours and tempts and perturbs the person he speaks to, and hinders him and leaves him in great unrest; and the more he communicates with him, the more he oppresses him and the further the man is from peace. Therefore it is God's will and to our profit that we recognize them apart; for God wants us always to be strong in our love, and peaceful and restful as he is towards us, and he wants us to be, for ourselves and for our fellow Christians, what he is for us. Amen.

Edmund Colledge and James Walsh, trans., *Julian of Norwich: Showings,* The Classics of Western Spirituality (New York: Paulist Press, 1978), 169-70.

FEAR

MARGARET EBNER

Once again in Advent I lay in bed at night. The greatest fear engulfed me so that I did not know what to do. Indeed, God helped me to fall asleep by the greatest grace. And I was in this grace when I awoke during the same night, but I can not speak about this state of mine. My Lord Jesus knows that well. Then I got up and felt grace for a long time afterward.

Leonard Hindsley, trans. and ed., *Margaret Ebner: Major Works,* The Classics of Western Spirituality (Mahwah, N.J.: Paulist Press, 1993), 94.

FRIENDSHIP

CATHERINE OF SIENA

[God says:] Now you have seen what a superb state they are in who have attained the love of friendship. They have mounted the feet of their affection and climbed as far as the secret of his heart, the second of the three stairs. I have told you the meaning of the soul's three powers, and now I would suggest to you that the stairs symbolize the three stages through which the soul advances.

But before I go on to the third stair I want to show you how a person comes to be my friend, and once my friend, becomes my child by attaining filial love. I want to show you what makes a person my friend and how you will know that you have become my friend.

First I will tell you how a soul comes to be my friend. In the beginning she was imperfect, living in slavish fear. By dint of practice and perseverance she came to the love of pleasure and self-advantage, because in me she found both pleasure and profit. This is the path those must travel who wish to attain perfect love, the love of friendship and filial love.

Filial love, I tell you, is perfect. For with filial love one receives the inheritance from me the eternal Father. But no one attains filial love without the love of friendship, and this is why I told you that one progresses from being my friend to becoming my child. But how does one come to this point? Let me tell you. Every perfection and every virtue proceeds from charity. Charity is nourished by humility. And humility comes from knowledge and holy hatred of oneself, that is, one's selfish sensuality. To attain charity you must dwell constantly in the cell of self-knowledge. For in knowing yourself you will come to know my mercy in the blood of my only-begotten Son, thus drawing my divine charity to yourself with your love. And you must exercise yourself in tearing out every perverse desire, whether spiritual or material, while you are hidden away within your house. This is what Peter and the other disciples did. For Peter wept after he had sinned in denying my Son. His weeping was still imperfect, though, and it remained imperfect for forty days, that is, till after the ascension.

After my Truth returned to me in his humanity, Peter and the others hid away at home and waited for the Holy Spirit to come as my Truth had promised he would. They remained locked up because of their fear. For the soul is always afraid until she has attained true love. But they persevered in watching and in constant humble prayer until they were filled with the Holy Spirit. Then they lost all their fear, and they followed and preached Christ crucified.

Suzanne Noffke, trans., *Catherine of Siena: The Dialogue,* The Classics of Western Spirituality (New York: Paulist Press, 1980), 118-19.

FRIENDSHIP

CATHERINE OF SIENA

[God says:] When a soul has reached the third stage, the love of friendship and filial love, her love is no longer mercenary. Rather she does as very close friends do when one receives a gift from the other. The receiver does not look just at the gift, but at the heart and the love of the giver, and accepts and treasures the gift only because of the friend's affectionate love. So the soul, when she has reached the third stage of perfect love, when she receives my gifts and graces and does not look only at the gift but with her mind's eye looks at the affectionate charity of me, the Giver.

And so that you might have no excuse for not looking at my affection, I found a way to unite gift and giver: I joined the divine nature with the human. I gave you the Word, my only-begotten Son, who is one with me and I with him, and because of this union you cannot look at my gift without looking at me, the Giver.

See, then, with what affectionate love you ought to love and desire both the gift and the giver! If you do, your love will be pure and genuine and not necessary. This is now it is with those who keep themselves always shut up in the house of self-knowledge.

Suzanne Noffke, trans., *Catherine of Siena: The Dialogue,* The Classics of Western Spirituality (New York: Paulist Press, 1980), 134.

FRIENDSHIP

MARGARET EBNER

I had a sister, whom God had given me for consolation in body and soul and who was very faithful to me. By divine design she served me joyfully throughout the years and protected me from all things that could disturb me. When, in my illness, I was sometimes unkind to her while she served me, she did not hold that against me. This sister became very ill by God's design. Then we were both sick and in suffering and patiently endured much pain. Because of that I was greatly distressed out of concern for my sister. I slept little every night due to sorrow, and still I desired to see her even in her suffering up to my own death. We were both weak and sick and suffering from the Assumption until St. Matthias Day of the next year. Then she died. The previous Christmas God had given me grace and strengthened me both outwardly and inwardly; outwardly by restoring my health, which was a wonder to me, and inwardly by profound recognition that all things were as nothing to me by comparison to God alone.

At the same time, while asleep, it was revealed to me how I should receive the Body of our Lord. When I drank from the chalice I perceived great sweetness, which I tasted for three days. I knelt before the altar after compline, and the grace was given me to realize that I must suffer, but also that God would help me in this suffering. I received that revelation from Him with much crying, and I fell down before Him and gave myself over to everything His grace was working in me. Soon after that, as the death of my sister approached, I saw and realized that she must die. I would gladly have died for her. She asked me to go away from her and to say my *Pater Noster,* because she knew well that whenever I said it, whatever burdened me would be made easier for me to bear. So I left her alone. I went away from her in great sorrow and recited my *Pater Noster,* and with the greatest yearning I commended us both to our dear Lord's works of love. Then I returned to her, but during the days that she still lingered I was in sorrow and misery although occasionally God would give me relief. I was with her all the time until she died. Then I went into choir with her body and read the psalter. Afterward I lay down and wanted to rest. As I lay there my heart was flooded with a very strong, very great light, with many graces and with much joy. I felt great joy in the thought that I should be suffering for God. Then I got up and went into choir again with great joy and read the psalter once more. When I saw her lying on the bier I found it hard to bear, despite the delight that I had even in my suffering. This delight lasted until prime when my usual sorrow overcame me again. When my sister died, I made a resolution to live in greater suffering from then on. I resolved, in particular, never to claim anything I needed as mine by necessity; instead I would take whatever was given to me, as if it were ordained for me by God.

Leonard Hindsley, trans. and ed., *Margaret Ebner: Major Works,* The Classics of Western Spirituality (Mahwah, N.J.: Paulist Press, 1993), 90-91.

FRIENDSHIP

TERESA OF AVILA

It is a great evil for a soul beset by so many dangers to be alone. I believe, if I had had anyone with whom to discuss all this, it would have helped me not to fall again, if only because I should have been ashamed in his sight, which I was not in the sight of God. For this reason I would advise those who practise prayer, especially at first, to cultivate friendship and intercourse with others of similar interests. This is a most important thing, if only because we can help each other by our prayers, and it is all the more so because it may bring us many other benefits. Since people can find comfort in the conversation and human sympathy of ordinary friendships, even when these are not altogether good, I do not know why anyone who is beginning to love and serve God in earnest should be allowed to his joys and trials with others—and people who practise prayer have plenty of both. For, if the friendship which such a person desires to have with His Majesty is true friendship, he need not be afraid of becoming vainglorious: as soon as the first motion of vainglory attacks him, he will repel it, and, in doing so, gain merit. I believe that anyone who discusses the subject with this in mind will profit both himself and his hearers, and will be all the wiser for it; and, without realizing he is doing so, will edify his friends.

E.Allison Peers, trans. and ed., *The Life of Teresa of Jesus: The Autobiography of Teresa of Avila* (New York: Image Books/Doubleday, 1991), 106-7.

FRIENDSHIP

TERESA OF AVILA

As I began to enjoy the good and holy conversation of this nun, I grew to delight in listening to her, for she spoke well about God and was very discreet and holy. There was never a time, I think, when I did not delight in listening to her words. She began to tell me how she had come to be a nun through merely reading those words in the Gospel: Many are called but few chosen. She used to describe to me the reward which the Lord gives to those who leave everything for His sake. This good companionship began to eradicate the habits which bad companionship had formed in me, to bring back my thoughts to desires for eternal things, and to remove some of the great dislike which I had for being a nun, and which had become deeply engrained in me. If I saw anyone weeping as she prayed, or giving evidence of any other virtues, I now greatly envied her; for my heart was so hard in this respect that, even if I read the entire narrative of the Passion, I could not shed a tear; and this distressed me.

E.Allison Peers, trans. and ed., *The Life of Teresa of Jesus: The Autobiography of Teresa of Avila* (New York: Image Books/Doubleday, 1991), 73-74

GOD

CATHERINE OF GENOA

In its creation the soul was endowed
with all the means necessary for coming to its
perfection,
for living as it ought to,
for not contaminating itself by sin.
Once sullied by sin, original and actual,
it loses those gifts and dies.
It can be brought back to life only by God.
The inclination to evil
still remains in the soul revivified by Baptism,
and unless it is strenuously fought leads back to death.
Afterwards,
God revivifies the soul with a special grace of His.
In no other way could the soul renounce its self-
centeredness
or return to the pristine state of its creation;
and as the soul makes its way to its first state,
its ardor in transforming itself into God is its purgatory,
the passionate instinct to overcome its impediments.
The last stage of love
is that which comes about and does its work without
man's doing.
If man were to be aware of the many hidden flaws in him
he would despair.
These flaws are burned away in the last stage of love.
God then shows that weakness to man,
so that the soul might see the workings of God,
of that flaming love.
Things man considers perfect
leave much to be desired in the eyes of God,
for all the things of man
that are perfect in appearance
—what he seeks, feels, knows—contaminate him.
If we are to become perfect,

the change must be brought about in us and without us;
that is, the change is to be the work not of man
but of God.
This, the last stage of love,
is the pure and intense love of God alone.
In this transformation,
the action of God in penetrating the soul is so fierce
that it seems to set the body on fire
and to keep it burning until death.
The overwhelming love of God
gives it a joy beyond words.

Serge Hughes, trans., *Catherine of Genoa: Purgation and Purgatory, The Spiritual Dialogue,* The Classics of Western Spirituality (New York: Paulist Press, 1979), 80-81.

GOD

CATHERINE OF GENOA

All this I saw as clearly as if I touched them,
but I cannot find the words to express them.
These things that I speak about work within me
in secret and with great power.
The prison in which I seem to be
is the world, the body its bonds;
and they weigh upon the lesser me within,
which is impeded from making its way to its true end.
To assist it in its weakness,
God's grace has allowed the soul
to participate in His life,
to become one with Him,
in the sharing of His goodness.
Since it is impossible for God to suffer,
the more souls immerse themselves in Him
the more they participate in His joyful Being.
Thus, the pain that remains is for the final
consummation,
the full actualization of the soul.

The more sinless the soul,
the more it knows and enjoys God,
in Whose presence it comes to rest.
He who would rather die than offend God
would still suffer the pangs of death;
he would be sustained, however, by the light of God,
Whom he honors.
Similarly, the soul, no matter how intense its sufferings,
values the ordinance of God above all things,
for He is above and beyond
whatever may be felt or conceived.
Such knowledge does not come through intellect or will,
as I have said. It comes from God, with a rush.
God busies the soul with Himself,
in no matter how slight a way,
and the soul, wrapped up in God,
cannot but be oblivious to all else.

Serge Hughes, trans., *Catherine of Genoa: Purgation and Purgatory, The Spiritual Dialogue,* The Classics of Western Spirituality (New York: Paulist Press, 1979), 86–87.

GOD

CATHERINE OF SIENA

For what would it mean to me to have eternal life if death were the lot of your people, or if my faults especially and those of your other creatures should bring darkness upon your bride, who is light itself? It is my will, then, and I beg it as a favor, that you have mercy on your people with the same eternal love that led you to create us in your image and likeness. And this you did, eternal Trinity, willing that we should share all that you are, high eternal Trinity! You, eternal Father, gave us memory to hold your gifts and share your power. You gave us understanding so that, seeing your goodness, we might share the wisdom of your only-begotten Son. And you gave us free will to love what our understanding sees and knows of your truth, and so share the mercy of your Holy Spirit.

Why did you so dignify us? With unimaginable love you looked upon your creatures within your very self, and you fell in love with us. So it was love that made you create us and give us being just so that we might taste your supreme eternal good.

Then I see how by our sin we lost the dignity you had given us. Rebels that we were, we declared war on your mercy and became your enemies. But stirred by the same fire that made you create us, you decided to give this warring human race a way to reconciliation, bringing great peace out of our war. So you gave us your only-begotten Son, your Word, to be mediator between us and you. He became our justice taking on himself the punishment for our injustices. He offered you the obedience you required of him in clothing him with our humanity, eternal Father, taking on our likeness and our human nature!

O depth of love! What heart could keep from breaking at the sight of your greatness descending to the lowliness of our humanity? We are your image, and now by making yourself one with us you have become our image, veiling your eternal divinity in the wretched cloud and dung heap of Adam. And why? For love! You, God, became human and we have been made divine! In the name of this unspeakable love, then, I beg you—I would force you even!—to have mercy on your creatures.

Suzanne Noffke, trans., *Catherine of Siena: The Dialogue,* The Classics of Western Spirituality (New York: Paulist Press, 1980), 49–50.

GOD

GERTRUDE THE GREAT OF HELFTA

In your extravagant generosity, kindest Lord, you added that if anyone knowing of the familiar companionship with which you have treated me, in my nothingness, during my lifetime, should humbly commend himself to my unworthy intercession after my death, you would without doubt deign to hear him as readily as you would ever grant the desire of anyone through the intercession of any other person; if, in reparation for his past negligence, he offer you thanks with humble devotion, especially for five graces:

The first is the love with which, in your merciful kindness, you chose me from all eternity. I can truthfully say that this is of all graces the most freely given. For you could not have been ignorant of how perverse my conduct would be, nor of all the details of my malice and wickedness and the baseness of my ingratitude. You might justly have denied me the honor due to human reason, even among pagans, but in your love which so greatly exceeds our misery you have chosen to confer on me, of all Christians, the dignity of being consecrated a religious.

The second is that you have drawn me to yourself for my salvation. And I am bound to confess that I owe this to the gentleness and goodness of your nature. You have won this rebellious heart (cf. Ez. 2:4) of mine (which in all justice deserves to be bound in iron chains), drawing it to yourself by your sweet caresses, as though you found in me a fit consort for your gentleness, and were quite delighted by your union with me.

The third is that you have so intimately united yourself with me. And this I can but attribute to your overflowing, immense, and boundless generosity. As though the number of the just were not sufficiently great to occupy your great love, you have called me, the least deserving of all, not in order to justify more easily the most suitable, but so that the miracle of your condescension might be reflected with great brilliance in the least suitable.

Fourth, that you should take pleasure in this union. This I can only ascribe to the folly of your love, if I may dare to speak in this way. As you have yourself asserted, you find your happiness in some incredible way in uniting your infinite wisdom with a being so unlike you and so unfitted for such a union.

Fifth, you are leading me graciously toward a blessed end. I humbly and firmly believe that I shall receive this gift from you, in the sweet kindness of your beneficent love, according to your faithful promise and despite my great unworthiness; and I embrace it with unshakable love and gratitude. It is not through any merit of mine, but solely through the free gift of your mercy, O my all, my supreme, my only true, eternal Good!

All these gifts are the effect of such astonishing conde-scension on your part and are so little in keeping with my misery that no thanksgiving of mine could ever be enough. Here, too, you have graciously deigned to come to my as-sistance, in my poverty, through the promises you have made to other souls whose thanksgiving may make good my deficiency. May praise and thanks be given to you by everything that is in heaven and earth and under the earth (cf. Phil. 2:10)!

Margaret Winkworth, trans. and ed., *Gertrude of Helfta: The Herald of Divine Love*, The Classics of Western Spirituality (Mahwah, N.J.: Paulist Press, 1993), 123-24.

GOD

HILDEGARD OF BINGEN

A wheel was shown to me, wonderful to behold.... Divin-ity is in its omniscience and omnipotence like a wheel, a circle, a whole, that can neither be understood, nor divided, nor begun nor ended.... Just as a circle embraces all that is within it, so does the Godhead embrace all.

Matthew Fox, *Illuminations of Hildegard of Bingen* (Santa Fe: Bear & Com-pany, 1985), 24.

GOD

HILDEGARD OF BINGEN

God hugs you. You are encircled by the arms of the mystery of God.

Matthew Fox, *Illuminations of Hildegard of Bingen* (Santa Fe: Bear & Company, 1985), 24.

GOD

HILDEGARD OF BINGEN

I am the breeze that nurtures all things green.
I encourage blossoms to flourish with ripening
     fruits.
I am the rain coming from the dew
that causes the grasses to laugh
with the joy of life.

Matthew Fox, *Illuminations of Hildegard of Bingen* (Santa Fe: Bear & Company, 1985), 33.

GOD

HILDEGARD OF BINGEN

I heard a voice from heaven say to me: "The all-powerful and ineffable God, who was before all ages but herself had no beginning nor will she cease to exist after the end of the ages—she it is who formed every creature in a marvelous way by her own will."

Matthew Fox, *Illuminations of Hildegard of Bingen* (Santa Fe: Bear & Company, 1985), 76.

God

HILDEGARD OF BINGEN

God created all things and ordained the human race for a glory which the devil, together with followers, lost. God should be worshipped and feared by all creatures with the greatest of honor and fear. It is just that worship be given by the creatures to the creator of all things and that God be adored most faithfully above all things. The very stone which you see does these things, for hidden in the stone is fear of God. God ought to spring up and always be present in all the intentions in the hearts of the faithful.

Indeed, you see an iron-colored stone which is very wide and high. This means that you should have strong, grand, and very great fear of God. God ought to be feared by every creature completely, for God is one and true, and no one is beyond or similar to God. God is very wide—as the stone—because God is incomprehensible in all things and above all things. God is very high, which means that no one is able to understand God's holy divinity. No one is able to reach up to God's divinity by stretching his or her own senses, because God's divinity is above all things. The stone is iron-colored. This means that it is burdensome and difficult for the human mind to fear God, for God is intensely heavy for the fragility of human dust—every human creature is a rebel to God.

... For wherever fear of God takes root, the wisdom of the human mind can be found. And God will help put faith in such a mind which God finds so satisfying. For when God is feared, God is known through the wisdom of a human mind which has faith. God is touched by such faith, just as a great lord is touched by the throne on which he sits. So God—who exists as the highest one above all things—finds rest in the faith which God has helped provide. God cannot be touched with power or with mastery, but only with singular and pure faith which believes God is above all things.

Bruce Hozeski, trans., *Hildegard von Bingen's Mystical Visions: Translated from Scivias,* introduced by Matthew Fox (Santa Fe: Bear & Company, 1995), 178-79.

GRACE

MARGARET EBNER

One time I was standing before the tabernacle and all the sisters wanted to receive our Lord. Then my heart was so full that I could not comprehend it. I thought it was as wide as the whole world. This happened often when I received our Lord. But sometimes I felt hardness from the thought that there was no sister who did not have more grace than I, and I was burdened heavily by that thought. Yet often God let me perceive grace later in the day or on the next day. Once, while I was sleeping, it seemed to me that I was in a choir with the sisters. Then I perceived grace and lightness so that it seemed to me that I beheld heaven on earth. Since then I have often experienced the same thing while awake. Whenever my life was shown to me while sleeping I took it as being true and have so perceived it ever since.

Leonard Hindsley, trans. and ed., *Margaret Ebner: Major Works,* The Classics of Western Spirituality (Mahwah, N.J.: Paulist Press, 1993), 89-90.

GRACE

MARGARET EBNER

I was still grieving for my sister, when God sent His true friend to the monastery around St. Narcissus Day. They asked me to go to him, but I went unwillingly because I still visited with no one and did not want to change. But when I visited him I listened gladly to his true teaching. I said little to him, and nothing to anyone else. This aroused fear in me that I did not love God as much as I claimed. Also I thought others spoke more profoundly than I and showed more devotion and love. I speak the truth when I say that I recognized myself as unworthy of all graces and gifts from God. By God's grace this well-prepared servant of God said to me, "Give me your sister." And I asked him, "Do you want her soul as well?" He answered, "What good is a body to me without a soul?" Then I received grace from his words so that the death of my sister was never again as unbearable as it had been.

Leonard Hindsley, trans. and ed., *Margaret Ebner: Major Works*, The Classics of Western Spirituality (Mahwah, N.J.: Paulist Press, 1993), 93.

HOLY SPIRIT

CATHERINE OF SIENA

[God says:] Such a soul has the Holy Spirit as a mother who nurses her at the breast of divine charity. The Holy Spirit has set her free, releasing her, as her lord, from the slavery of selfish love. For where the fire of my charity is, the water of selfishness cannot enter to put out this sweet fire in the soul. This servant, the Holy Spirit, whom I in my providence have given her, clothes her, nurtures her, inebriates her with tenderness and the greatest wealth. Because she has left all she finds all. Because she has stripped herself of herself she is clothed in me. She has made herself the servant of all in humility, so now she is made mistress over the world and her own sensuality. Because she became blind in her own sight she is now in perfect light. Because she put no trust in herself she is crowned with living faith and fulfilled hope. She has a taste of eternal life, free of every distressing pain and bitterness. She judges all things rightly because in all things she discerns my will. She has seen by the light of faith that I will nothing other than her holiness, and this has made her patient.

Suzanne Noffke, trans., *Catherine of Siena: The Dialogue*, The Classics of Western Spirituality (New York: Paulist Press, 1980), 292.

HOLY SPIRIT

HILDEGARD OF BINGEN

O Holy Spirit, Fiery Comforter Spirit, Life of the life of all creatures. Who is the Holy Spirit? The Holy Spirit is a Burning Spirit. It kindles the hearts of humankind. Like tympanum and lyre it plays them, gathering volumes in the temple of the soul. . . . The Holy Spirit resurrects and awakens everything that is.

Matthew Fox, *Illuminations of Hildegard of Bingen* (Santa Fe: Bear & Company, 1985), 9.

HOLY SPIRIT

HILDEGARD OF BINGEN

The Holy Spirit streams through and ties together "eternity" and "equality" so that they are one. This is like someone tying a bundle together—for there would be no bundle if it weren't tied together—everything would fall apart.

Matthew Fox, *Illuminations of Hildegard of Bingen* (Santa Fe: Bear & Company, 1985), 23.

HOLY SPIRIT

HILDEGARD OF BINGEN

Truly,
the Holy Spirit is an unquenchable fire.

He bestows all excellence,
    sparks all worth,
    awakes all goodness,
    ignites speech,
    enflames humankind.

Yet in this radiance is a restorative
    stillness.
It is the stillness that is similarly
in the will to good.
It spreads to all sides.

The Holy Spirit, then,
through one's fervent longings,
pours the juice of contrition
into the hardened human heart.

Holy Spirit,
All creation praises you.
Creation has life because of you.
You are precious salve for broken bones,
    for festering wounds.
You transform them to precious gems.
Now gather us together in your praise.
Lead us on the proper path.

In the aimless, spinning soul
where fog obscures the intellect and will,
where the fruit is noxious and poisonous,
you guide the pruning sword.

Thus the spirit orders all desire.

But should the soul
incline to be covetous and incorrigible,
fixing its gaze on evil's face,
looking ever with eyes of malice,
you rush in with fire,
and burn,
as you will.

Gabriele Uhlein, *Meditations with Hildegard of Bingen* (Santa Fe: Bear & Company, 1983), 38–39.

Holy Spirit

Hildegard of Bingen

*He carried me in spirit to the top of a great and high
mountain. And he showed me the holy city Jerusalem
which was coming down from heaven. It gleamed with
the brightness of God (Revelation 21:10-11).* This can be
interpreted in the following way. The Spirit lifts up the spirit.
How does the Spirit do this? With its virtues, the Holy Spirit
lifts up the minds of people from the weight of their flesh.
Then they can fly within the sight of the eyes of the Spirit
who sees inner things, since they are no longer darkened
by the blindness of their fleshly desires. What does this
mean? The Holy Spirit lifts the spirits of people upward to
the mountain of heavenly desires so that they can be strong
enough to clearly contemplate the works of God. For the
thousand crafts of the devil have drawn people down, so
that people are dominated by them as a mountain domi-
nates the level ground upon the earth. Indeed the Holy
Spirit is a solid foundation and is just like a mountain which
does not move from its place. And a mountain has such
great height that the mortal senses of people cannot explain it. It goes beyond every human discretion, and it
mounts above earthly minds which are even of great earthly
quality.

Therefore, the faithful and holy souls are shown the
works of the Holy Spirit. And they ought to build the heavenly Jerusalem spiritually with the gifts from the Holy Spirit
rather than with the work of fleshly hands. With the greatness and the height of these gifts in their spirits, they ought
to embellish the heavenly Jerusalem with the good works
which have been made with the touch of the Holy Spirit.

Bruce Hozeski, trans., *Hildegard von Bingen's Mystical Visions: Translated from Scivias,* introduced by Matthew Fox (Santa Fe: Bear & Company, 1995), 341-42.

HUMILITY

CATHERINE OF SIENA

[God says:] The first is that you must all be enlightened to know the transitory things of this world, that they all pass away like the wind. But you cannot know this well unless you first know your own weakness, how ready that perverse law bound up in your members makes you to rebel against me your Creator. Not that this law can force any one of you to commit the least sin unless you want to, but it certainly does fight against the spirit. Nor did I give this law so that my people should be conquered, but so that they might increase and prove virtue in their souls. For virtue can be proved only by its opposite. Sensuality is the opposite of the spirit, so it is through sensuality that the soul proves the love she has for me her Creator. When does she prove it? When she mounts hatred and contempt against it.

I gave the soul this law also to keep her truly humble. So you see, while I created her in my image and likeness and made her so honorable and beautiful, I gave her as well the vilest thing there is, this perverse law. In other words, I bound her into a body formed from the vilest earth so that when she saw her beauty she would not lift up her head in pride against me. So the weak body is a reason for humility to those who have this light [of mine]. They have no reason at all to be proud, but they do have reason for true and perfect humility. This perverse law, then, no matter how it fights, cannot force the least sin. Rather it is reason for you to learn to know yourself and to know how inconstant is the world.

Suzanne Noffke, trans., *Catherine of Siena: The Dialogue,* The Classics of Western Spirituality (New York: Paulist Press, 1980), 185.

HUMILITY

CLARE OF ASSISI

Truly I can rejoice—and no one can rob me of such joy—
6. since, having at last what under heaven I have desired, I
see that, helped by a special gift of wisdom from the mouth
of God Himself and in an awe-inspiring and unexpected
way, you have brought to ruin the subtleties of our crafty
enemy, the pride that destroys human nature, and the vanity that infatuates human hearts. 7. [I see, too] that by humility, the virtue of faith, and the strong arms of poverty,
you have taken hold of that *incomparable treasure hidden in the field* of the world and of the human heart (cf.
Mt 13:44), with which you have purchased that by Whom
all things have been made from nothing. 8. And, to use the
words of the Apostle himself in their proper sense, I consider you a *co-worker of God* Himself (cf. 1 Cor 3:9; Rm
16:3) and a support of the weak members of His ineffable
Body.

9. Who is there, then, who would not encourage me to
rejoice over such marvelous joys? 10. Therefore, dearly beloved, may you too *always rejoice in the Lord* (Phil 4:4).
11. And may neither bitterness nor a cloud [of sadness]
overwhelm you, o dearly beloved Lady in Christ, joy of the
angels and crown of your sisters!

12. Place your mind before the mirror of eternity!
Place your soul *in the brilliance of glory!*
13. Place your heart *in the figure of the* divine *substance!*
And *transform* your entire being *into the image*
of the Godhead Itself through contemplation.

14. So that you too may feel what His friends feel
as they taste *the hidden sweetness*
that God Himself has reserved from the beginning
for those who love Him.

15. And, after all who ensnare their blind lovers
   in a deceitful and turbulent world
   have been completely sent away,
   you may totally love Him
   Who gave Himself totally for your love. . . .

18. May you cling to His most sweet Mother who gave
birth to a Son whom the heavens could not contain. . . .
20. Who would not dread the treacheries of the enemy
of humanity who, through the arrogance of momentary and
deceptive glories, attempts to reduce to nothing that which
is greater than heaven itself? 21. Indeed, it is now clear
that the soul of a faithful person, the most worthy of all
creatures because of the grace of God, is greater than
heaven itself, 22. since the heavens and the rest of creation
cannot contain their Creator and only the faithful soul is
His dwelling place and throne, and this only through the
charity that the wicked lack. 23. [He Who is] the Truth has
said: Whoever loves me will be loved by My Father, and I
too shall love him, and We shall come to him and make
Our dwelling place with him (Jn 14:21, 23).

Regis Armstrong, ed., *Clare of Assisi: Early Documents* (New York: Paulist Press,
1988), 44-45.

HUMILITY

GERTRUDE THE GREAT OF HELFTA

The conversations she held with the Lord of majesty were
so substantial that we knew of no one who matched her in
our generation; yet their effect was always to lead her to
greater humility. She used to say that as long as she kept all
that she had received from God's overflowing goodness to
herself, and enjoyed it in isolation, unworthy of the grace
and ungrateful for it, it all seemed to her to be lying hidden
in dung, because of her worthlessness. But when she had
communicated it to someone else, then she thought of it

as a precious stone in a gold setting, for she considered everyone to be worthier than herself. She reckoned that everyone else, because of their spotless and worthy lives, could give God greater praise by a single thought than she could accomplish, because of her unworthy life and carelessness, by the full exertion of her body. This alone compelled her to expose anything God bestowed on her to all and sundry, because she judged herself so completely unworthy of all God's gifts that she could not possibly believe that they had been given her for herself alone, but rather for the salvation of others.

Alexander Barratt, trans., *Gertrud the Great of Helfta: The Herald of God's Loving-Kindness* (Kalamazoo, Mich.: Cistercian Publications, 1991), 51.

HUMILITY

GERTRUDE THE GREAT OF HELFTA

Among her many glowing virtues, shining like twinkling stars, with which the Lord had made her extraordinarily beautiful as a dwelling-place for himself, humility in particular shone out—humility the refuge of all graces and the guardian of all virtues. Persuaded by humility, she considered herself so unworthy of all God's gifts that there was no way she could agree to receive a gift to her own advantage. She thought of herself as a channel through which grace might flow to those whom God had chosen, as the result of some hidden design of God's, since she was herself so completely unworthy and received all God' gifts, the greatest and the least, without the least merit or profit. The only merit she could claim was that she labored to give them away, through what she wrote or said, for the good of her neighbor. This she did with such faithfulness toward God and humility toward herself that again and again she would say to herself, "Even if after this I am tormented in hell, as I deserve, nonetheless I am glad that the Lord will then gather in others the fruit of his gifts." She acknowledged no one so worthless, in whom she did not think God's gift more profitably invested than in herself. Nonetheless, she never flinched from being ready for any of God's gifts at any time, and consequently was always ready to dispense them for the advantage of her neighbors, as if they belonged less to her than to others who received them through her mediation.

Passing judgment on herself in the light of truth, she saw herself as the most distant among those of whom the prophet says: "All nations are as nothing in his sight" and earlier, "Like a speck of dust" and so forth. For just as a speck of dust lying under a twig or some such thing is hidden from the sun's rays by a sliver of shadow, so she by effacing herself did all that she could to deflect the excellence of such noble gifts of God, and to accept those gifts only because he who offered them precedes by his inspiration those whom he calls, and follows with his help those whom he justifies. For herself she retained only the guilt which, so she thought, she revealed in being so ungrateful for, and so unworthy of, such freely-given gifts. But with his glory in mind she could not keep silent about God's loving-kindness toward her. She was careful to bring it to the notice of others with this intention in her heart: "It is quite wrong for God's goodness toward me not to produce better fruit in others than it can produce in me, an abandoned and utterly worthless creature."

Alexander Barratt, trans., *Gertrud the Great of Helfta: The Herald of God's Loving-Kindness* (Kalamazoo, Mich.: Cistercian Publications, 1991), 70–71.

HUMILITY

GERTRUDE THE GREAT OF HELFTA

On the feast of St. Matthew, Apostle, God came to meet her with great blessings of sweetness. At the elevation of the chalice she was offering this same chalice as a thanksgiving to the Lord; and she began to reflect in her heart that her offering of the aforesaid chalice would not be complete unless she offered herself to endure tribulations for Christ. And so, in this state of holy elation, she tore herself away from the place where she seemed to be reclining delightfully on the Lord's breast and threw herself down on the ground, like a wretched corpse, with these words: "Lord, I offer myself to bear everything that may be to your praise!" The Lord at once made haste to rise and, lying down on the ground beside her, as if gathering her to himself, he said: "This is my own!" As though revived by the virtue of the divine presence, she raised herself up before the Lord and said: "Yea, my Lord, I am the work of your hands." And the Lord said: "You have received this further grace because my love is so intertwined with you that I could not live in complete blessedness without you." Marveling at the excessive condescension of these words, she said: "O my Lord, why do you speak thus, since having deigned to find your delight in your creatures (cf. Prov. 8:31), you have an infinite number of others, both on earth and in heaven, with whom you could live in complete blessedness, even had I never been created?" To which the Lord replied: "He who has always lacked a limb does not suffer the same affliction as someone who has one of his limbs cut off when already an adult. So, from the moment I set my love upon you, I could never suffer us to be separated from one another."

Margaret Winkworth, trans. and ed., *Gertrude of Helfta: The Herald of Divine Love*, The Classics of Western Spirituality (Mahwah, N.J.: Paulist Press, 1993), 159-60.

Humility

Hadewijch of Antwerp (Brabant)

Then he led me farther to where a tree stood that was very low and had beautiful leaves, graceful and multicolored, that were pleasing to the sight. And above all these beautiful leaves hung withered leaves that concealed all the beautiful leaves. And then the Angel said again: "Chosen soul of high aspirations, you have been drawn from such ignobility to such loftiness, from such dark ignorance to such light (cf. 1 Pet. 2:9), and from such great poverty to the greatest wealth—understand what this is!" And he showed me, and I understood that it was humility that had recognized God's greatness and its own unworthiness, and now with wise fear hid all the virtues by which it was truly adorned, because it felt and knew that it lacked fruition of its Beloved, and that it did not know how to remedy this lack. This is pure humility.

Mother Columba Hart, trans., *Hadewijch: The Complete Works*, The Classics of Western Spirituality (New York: Paulist Press, 1980), 264.

Humility

Hildegard of Bingen

Humility caused the Word of God to be born from the Virgin, where humility was neither in envious surroundings, nor in the beauty of the flesh, nor in earthly riches, nor in golden ornaments, nor in worldly honors. But the Word of God was placed in a manger because the Word's mother was poor. Furthermore, humility always sighs and destroys all crimes because that is its work. Whenever the devil wishes to capture something, that object should protect and arm itself with humility because Lucifer certainly fled from humility, even as the serpent hides itself in a cave whenever humility is present. Wherever humility seized the serpent, it very quickly shattered the serpent as if it were a worthless thread.

Bruce Hozeski, trans., *Hildegard von Bingen's Mystical Visions: Translated from Scivias,* introduced by Matthew Fox (Santa Fe: Bear & Company, 1995), 24-25.

HUMILITY

HILDEGARD OF BINGEN

Dispose of your treasure as the Most High commands, for that will profit you more than the gold (Sirach 29:11). What does this mean?

Having thought justly and rightly, take your reward, which is in your bosom and in your heart. Divide it up according to God's commands because God commanded you to turn away from evil and to do good. You ought to overflow with generousity in your breast, so that you are not with the lost sheep, but with God. Yield yourself to God, and honor God with things *from your substance (Proverbs 3:9),* because God will then have mercy on you in your miseries. If you have done these things, your compassion will prove very useful. Have compassion on those who possess no treasures. Do not take pride in your compassion, as if it were a great treasure of gold. For it is better for you to give a small amount in humility than it is for you to have the kingdom of the world with pleasure. God's mercy might fail you then, because of the weight of your pride. For you did not have compassion upon the poor.

Bruce Hozeski, trans., *Hildegard von Bingen's Mystical Visions: Translated from Scivias,* introduced by Matthew Fox (Santa Fe: Bear & Company, 1995), 152-53.

HUMILITY

HILDEGARD OF BINGEN

I am humility, the column of humble minds and the murderess of proud hearts. I began in the least of places, but I have ascended to the lofty place of the heavens. Lucifer lifted Lucifer upwards, but fell downwards. Whoever wishes to imitate me and desires to be my child, and if that person wants to embrace me as if I were his or her mother by doing my work in me, let this person touch the foundation and then gently lift himself or herself upwards to the top. What does this mean? Let this person think about the worthlessness of his or her own flesh, and let this person climb step by step upwards *from virtue to virtue (Psalm 84:8)* with a sweet and gentle soul. For whoever climbs first to the highest branch of a tree, that person most often falls unexpectedly. But whoever begins by climbing from the base of the tree, that person will not fall so easily if he or she proceeds cautiously.

Bruce Hozeski, trans., *Hildegard von Bingen's Mystical Visions: Translated from Scivias,* introduced by Matthew Fox (Santa Fe: Bear & Company, 1995), 278.

HUMILITY

MARGUERITE PORETE

You who would read this book,
If you indeed wish to grasp it,
Think about what you say,
For it is very difficult to comprehend;
Humility, who is keeper of the treasury of
Knowledge
And the mother of the other Virtues,
Must overtake you.

Theologians and other clerks,
You will not have the intellect for it,
No matter how brilliant your abilities,
If you do not proceed humbly.
And may Love and Faith, together,
Cause you to rise above Reason,
[Since] they are the ladies of the house.

Even Reason witnesses
In the Thirteenth Chapter of this book,
And with no shame about it,
That Love and Faith make her live
And she does not free herself from them,
For they have lordship over her,
Which is why she must humble herself.

Humble, then, your wisdom
Which is based on Reason,
And place all your fidelity
In those things which are given
By Love, illuminated through Faith.
And thus you will understand this book
Which makes the Soul live by love.

Ellen L. Babinsky, trans., *Marguerite Porete: The Mirror of Simple Souls*, The Classics of Western Spirituality (Mahwah, N.J.: Paulist Press, 1993), 79.

HUMILITY

TERESA OF AVILA

I only wish I could write with both hands, so as not to forget one thing while I am saying another.
From foolish devotions may God deliver us.

E. Allison Peers, trans. and ed., *The Life of Teresa of Jesus: The Autobiography of Teresa of Avila* (New York: Image Books/Doubleday, 1991), 17.

HUMILITY

TERESA OF AVILA

The authority of persons so learned and serious as my confessors suffices for the approval of any good thing that I may say, if the Lord gives me grace to say it, in which case it will not be mine but His; for I have no learning, nor have I led a good life, nor do I get my information from a learned man or from any other person whatsoever. Only those who have commanded me to write this know that I am doing so, and at the moment they are not here. I am almost stealing the time for writing, and that with great difficulty, for it hinders me from spinning and I am living in a poor house and have numerous things to do.

E. Allison Peers, trans. and ed., *The Life of Teresa of Jesus: The Autobiography of Teresa of Avila* (New York: Image Books/Doubleday, 1991), 41–42.

HUMILITY

TERESA OF AVILA

Well now let's get back to our castle with its many dwelling places. You mustn't think of these dwelling places in such a way that each one would follow in file after the other; but turn your eyes toward the center, which is the room or royal chamber where the King stays, and think of how a palmetto has many leaves surrounding and covering the tasty part that can be eaten. So here, surrounding this center room are many other rooms; and the same holds true for those above. The things of the soul must always be considered as plentiful, spacious, and large; to do so is not an exaggeration. The soul is capable of much more than we can imagine, and the sun that is in this royal chamber shines in all parts. It is very important for any soul that practices prayer, whether little or much, not to hold itself back and stay in one corner. Let it walk through these dwelling places which are up above, down below, and to the sides, since God has given it such great dignity. Don't force it to stay a long time in one room alone. Oh, but if it is in the room of self-knowledge! How necessary this room is—see that you understand me—even for those whom the Lord has brought into the very dwelling place where He abides. For never, however exalted the soul may be, is anything else more fitting than self-knowledge; nor could it be even were the soul to so desire. For humility, like the bee making honey in the beehive, is always at work. Without it, everything goes wrong. But let's remember that the bee doesn't fail to leave the beehive and fly about gathering nectar from the flowers. So it is with the soul in the room of self-knowledge; let it believe me and fly sometimes to ponder the grandeur and majesty of its God.

Here it will discover its lowliness better than by thinking of itself, and be freer from the vermin that enter the first rooms, those of self-knowledge. For even though, as I say, it is by the mercy of God that a person practices self-knowledge, that which applies to what is less applies so much more to what is greater, as they say. And believe me, we shall practice much better virtue through God's help than by being tied down to our own misery.

I don't know if this has been explained well. Knowing ourselves is something so important that I wouldn't want any relaxation ever in this regard, however high you may have climbed into the heavens. While we are on this earth nothing is more important to us than humility. So I repeat that it is good, indeed very good, to try to enter first into the room where self-knowledge is dealt with rather than fly off to other rooms. This is the right road, and if we can journey along a safe and level path, why should we want wings to fly? Rather, let's strive to make more progress in self-knowledge, for in my opinion we shall never completely know ourselves if we don't strive to know God. By gazing at His grandeur, we get in touch with our own lowliness; by looking at His purity, we shall see our own filth; by pondering His humility, we shall see how far we are from being humble.

Kieran Kavanaugh and Otilio Rodriguez, trans., *Teresa of Avila: The Interior Castle*, The Classics of Western Spirituality (New York: Paulist Press, 1979), 42–43.

JESUS CHRIST

ANGELA OF FOLIGNO

One day I was meditating on the dreadful pains Christ endured on the cross. I was considering the nails which, as I had heard it said, had pressed the flesh of his hands and feet into the wood. And I wanted to see at least that small amount of Christ's flesh that had been pressed into the wood. This torture of Christ gave me such great sorrow that I could no longer stand on my feet. I bent over and sat down. I stretched out my arms on the ground and inclined my head on them. Then Christ showed me his breast and arms. Then my sorrow changed into a joy so intense I can say nothing of it. It was a joy different from any other. I could see, hear, feel nothing but it. There was so much light within my soul that I have no more doubt and will ask no further question. And he left this sign of joy with so much certainty in my soul that I believe I will never lose it. His breast and his neck were so beautiful I realized such beauty was divine. Hence, because of that beauty, it seemed to me I was seeing his divinity, and that I was standing in the presence of God—but nothing else was shown to me besides this. I cannot compare this illumination with any object or color of the world, except perhaps with the light of Christ's body, which I sometimes see at the elevation.

José De Vinck, *Revelations of Women Mystics: From Middle Ages to Modern Times* (New York: Alba House, 1985), 52.

JESUS CHRIST

HILDEGARD OF BINGEN

While humankind
was being beguiled
by the advice of the snake,

I made my passionate appearance.

In the enkindled womb of the virgin
I came to rest.
I became human in her flesh.

After I came forth
from the virgin's womb,
I brought humankind home again
in the waters of baptism
through which I purified
the human seed.

Gabriele Uhlein, *Meditations with Hildegard of Bingen* (Santa Fe: Bear & Company, 1983), 114.

JESUS CHRIST

JULIAN OF NORWICH

God rejoices in that he is our Mother. . . .

The deep wisdom of the Trinity is our Mother, in whom we are enclosed. . . .

God All-Wisdom is our Mother. . . .

The Second Person of the Trinity is our Mother by nature, in our substantial making. In it, we are grounded and rooted, and it is our Mother by mercy in our bodies, by incarnation. . . .

Thus Jesus Christ, who does good as opposed to evil, is our true Mother: we receive our being from him in whom the ground of motherhood begins with all the sweet preservation of love that follows without end. . . . "I am It, the Wisdom and Nature of Motherhood."

José De Vinck, *Revelations of Women Mystics: From Middle Ages to Modern Times* (New York: Alba House, 1985), 73.

JESUS CHRIST

MARGARET EBNER

It was on a Friday night and I had been to visit the graves. As I went into choir a sweet fragrance surrounded me and penetrated through my heart and into all my limbs and the name Jesus Christus was given to me so powerfully that I could pay attention to nothing else. And it seemed to me that I was really in His presence. I experienced such great grace that I could not pull myself away. Then a holy sister named Adelheid, whom God gave me after my sister had died, came in and wanted to pray. I went up to her and, since I kept silence during the day, made a sign to her wanting to know whether she noticed the fragrance. She could not understand me and I was frightened by this and understood well that she did not perceive it. I left her and said nothing to her about it until the day when I began to speak again. I perceived the fragrance for three days in the choir. As to all events in the monastery I paid as little attention to them as if they were happening in another monastery.

Leonard Hindsley, trans. and ed., *Margaret Ebner: Major Works,* The Classics of Western Spirituality (Mahwah, N.J.: Paulist Press, 1993), 93.

Jesus Christ

Margaret Ebner

This was revealed to me in that year: whenever I heard something about our Lord, especially when I heard the Name of Jesus Christ, I was inwardly grasped and so filled up by the grace of God and by divine sweetness that I sat there a long time and did not move externally and could not speak a word.

My conscience was not burdened by the sorrowful condition of Christianity, but often I had to go without the Eucharist. Our Order has never submitted to the commands, as others have done. Although our monastery was still bound by the law, we were permitted to act according to our consciences here. All the while this conviction stood firm in my heart: if I knew that by receiving holy communion or by going to Mass I acted against God, I would rather die than act in such way. I placed this before the faithfulness of Our Lord and said, "Lord, if you let me do something wrong here, then you must do penance for me." God answered me, "You should come to me, because I will never leave you, neither here nor hereafter. Whoever desires me in true love, I will never renounce out of true love." I speak in the Truth, who is my Lord Jesus Christ, that the grace of God has never decreased in me because of this. At that time great grace was given to me by God when I received our Lord on such great feast days as Pentecost and the feast of our Lady, All Saints, St. John's Day, and also for all of Advent and on Christmas Day.

My Lord, who is pure Truth, knows well that since that time I have withdrawn myself as much as is humanly possible in thought, word, and deed from all things that are opposed to God.

My Lord Jesus Christ in His goodness has also given me this: when midnight approaches keeping vigil is no burden for me and never causes me to become ill. During the vigil God gives me the most joyful, human peace, which strengthens me both inwardly and outwardly. It comes upon me with a feeling of lightness and ends in joy. The whole day I feel an increase of divine grace and bodily strength. Sometimes I look up and see little white lights before me, so that I think day is dawning. But indeed it is not yet day and the shutters are still closed. Then I see the altar and the walls in the cell and myself. This is given to me as an image of the peace which God has with loving delight in the loving soul, and that same delight the loving soul has for Him.

Leonard Hindsley, trans. and ed., *Margaret Ebner: Major Works*, The Classics of Western Spirituality (Mahwah, N.J.: Paulist Press, 1993), 104–5.

JESUS CHRIST

MARGARET EBNER

My Truth, Jesus Christ, knows well that nothing in this world is sweeter or more delightful to me than the Name *Jesus Christus*. With it I am lovingly compelled and pressed into the suffering of my dearly Beloved Jesus Christ; by it arises from within me the most wonderful fragrance; in it I feel the sweetest grace with great power. Especially during my *Pater Noster* it often becomes more forceful by strong, mysterious grace that is beyond my human senses. I thought that I could not finish my *Pater Noster* alive due to the overflow of grace. It is so well with me then that I think, "Can heaven be better than this?" My human understanding cannot grasp this. Such a powerful love and such a strong faith are given to me that I perceive God's presence as real, so that all things become delightful. Even at the thought of hell I have no fear because the presence of God could be as little taken from me there as in heaven. Then great delight in God overwhelms me.

Leonard Hindsley, trans. and ed., *Margaret Ebner: Major Works*, The Classics of Western Spirituality (Mahwah, N.J.: Paulist Press, 1993), 108.

JESUS CHRIST

MARGARET EBNER

In particular, very sweet grace was given me by God in my love for His beloved disciple, my lord St. John. Whenever I remembered how my lord, St. John, rested upon the dear heart of my Lord Jesus Christ, such sweet grace stirred in me that I could not speak a word. When I recalled the sweet drink he drank and sucked from the sweet breast of Christ, again I could not speak at all, and I sat there with delight and desire so that I would have gladly died out of love. And when I desired that this be given to me too, just as he had received it, then I was so moved again that I had to sit a while. This was given to me last year in Advent and has intensified this year. Whenever I remembered this and the intense desire I was not able to say the words well, but I was moved inwardly and I sat there longer. It gave me a sweet inner joy in God and a powerful grasp of truth whenever very hidden things were given to me which I had neither desired nor could desire. Then I felt, in the fullness of grace, that no one can give this except God alone.

Leonard Hindsley, trans. and ed., *Margaret Ebner: Major Works,* The Classics of Western Spirituality (Mahwah, N.J.: Paulist Press, 1993), 125.

JUSTICE

GERTRUDE THE GREAT OF HELFTA

Justice, that is to say, the zeal of burning charity, which St. Bernard ... calls the sun of the soul, shone in her with such brightness that if occasion had called upon her to fight in its defense, she would have faced the armed battalions of a thousand armies drawn up in battle array (cf. Song 6:3–9). There was no friend, however dear, whom she would have consented to defend against the most deadly of foes, not even by a single word, if it meant straying from the paths of justice. She would have preferred to see her own mother harmed (if right reason demanded it) rather than consent to any injustice, even toward the most troublesome of enemies.

Margaret Winkworth, trans. and ed., *Gertrude of Helfta: The Herald of Divine Love*, The Classics of Western Spirituality (Mahwah, N.J.: Paulist Press, 1993), 63.

JUSTICE

HILDEGARD OF BINGEN

At every hour of the day you should think about how you received so great a gift and how you have made it go to work for yourself and for others and how you might give it back in your works for justice. In doing so you are giving back the splendor of holiness because other people, called forth by your good example, might show forth honor and praise to God. Because when you multiply these gifts by using them in every way for justice, then praise and action of giving thanks will make God known. And it is God who breathed these virtues into you by the Holy Spirit in the first place.

Matthew Fox, *Illuminations of Hildegard of Bingen* (Santa Fe: Bear & Company, 1985), 99.

JUSTICE

HILDEGARD OF BINGEN

When a person understands Justice
the self is let go.

The just taste and drink virtue.
This strengthens them, as if
they were addicted to wine,
yet they are never beside
themselves,
are never uncontrollable,
or know not what they do,
as is the case with drunkards.

The just love God,
of whom there can be no surfeit,
only utter, constant ecstacy.

The first seed of the longing for Justice
blows through the soul like the wind.

The taste for good will plays in it
like a breeze.

The consummation of this seed
is a greening in the soul
that is like that
of the ripening world.

Now the soul honors God
by the doing of just deeds.

The soul is only as strong as its works.

Gabriele Uhlein, *Meditations with Hildegard of Bingen* (Santa Fe: Bear & Company, 1983), 122–23.

JUSTICE

HILDEGARD OF BINGEN

This image which was leaning on the columns stands for the justice of God. She is limited after wisdom in all her own justices among people by the Holy Spirit. She was of such breadth that she might be compared to the breadth of five men standing side by side. This signifies that she is the expansion of the capacity of the five senses in humans. She turns them around to the breadth of the law of God. And she surrounds and protects the precepts of life established by God in the ones choosing her. She was of such great height that I was not able to discern it perfectly. She was so tall that she could look out through all of the building. This means that she goes beyond the human intellect in her own height. She stretches upwards to heavenly things so that she also *looked out from heaven (Psalm 85:12)* at the time of the incarnation of the savior when the savior—of course, the Word of God—went forth from God who had brought forth true justice. She also directed her sight into the tools of the church at this time. For those tools are made in her and contained in her, just as the higher ramparts are joined to the very strong tower through which they are able to stand firm. She had such a great head and such clear eyes that she could see most keenly into heaven. This refers to the fact that the greatest and highest goodness of justice showed people the brightest of visions in the incarnation of the Word of God when the Word was made manifest in a human body to earthly and darkened eyes. Justice then gazed at heavenly things at the time of the redemption of souls. And she appeared all white and was as bright as a very bright cloud. This means that she dwells in the whiteness and purity of the minds of just people. Such people stretch with all their zeal so that they may be placed most faithfully under the justice of God. She makes herself like clouds as she prepares a suitable dwelling place for herself in the hearts of just people. I saw, however, no further likeness to a person in her. This means that she remains in heavenly things and not in worldly things—as it has been shown to you. People do not cling to her because they are burdened with human work, but human work does justify their life. But God is just, and she—being opposed to the devil—urges the other virtues to do the work of God. She showed this faithfully above.

Bruce Hozeski, trans., *Hildegard von Bingen's Mystical Visions: Translated from Scivias*, introduced by Matthew Fox (Santa Fe: Bear & Company, 1995), 314–15.

Love

ANGELA OF FOLIGNO

There is nothing in the world, neither man nor devil nor any thing, that I hold as suspect as love, for it penetrates the soul more than any other thing. Nothing exists that so fills and binds the heart as love does. Therefore, unless you have the weapons to regulate it, love can easily make the soul fall into utter ruin. I am not speaking about evil love, which of course all must shun as dangerous and a thing of the devil, but about good and spiritual love between God and the soul, neighbor and neighbor.

It often happens that two or three people, men and women, love one another very intensely and harbor such heartfelt and special affection for one another that they want to be almost always together. Whatever one wishes, the other also wishes. Unless it is regulated with the weapons just mentioned, this type of love is very reprehensible and dangerous, even if it is spiritual and conceived for God's sake. For if the love the soul has for God is not forearmed it will be swept away by its own fervor, soon decrease or fall into some disorder, and not be able to last. Unless it is regulated by the proper weapons, true love of neighbor, that of devout men and women, either becomes carnal or gets lost in wasted conversations. For hearts bound to one another in this type of imperfect love are extremely indiscreet. This is why for fear of wrongful love, I am willing to suspect the love that is good.

Paul Lachance, trans., *Angela of Foligno: Complete Works,* The Classics of Western Spirituality (Mahwah, N.J.: Paulist Press, 1993), 221.

LOVE

ANGELA OF FOLIGNO

Love has various properties. Because of love, and in it, the soul first grows tender, then it pines and grows weak, and afterward finds strength. When the soul feels the heat of divine love, it cries out and moans. It is like a stone flung in the forge to melt it into lime; it crackles when it is licked by the flames, but after it is baked makes not a sound. Thus the soul in the beginning seeks divine consolations, but if these are withdrawn, it grows tender, and even cries out against God and complains to him: "You are hurting me! Why are you doing this?" and so forth. Assurance of God's presence engenders tenderness in the soul. In this state it is satisfied with consolations and other similar gifts. But in the absence of these, love grows and begins to seek the loved one. If it does not find him, the soul pines. It is then no longer satisfied with consolations, for it seeks only the Beloved. The more the soul receives consolations and feels God, the more its love grows, but the more, likewise, it pines in the absence of the Beloved.

But once the soul is perfectly united to God, it is placed in the seat of truth, for truth is the seat of the soul. It then no longer cries out nor complains about God, nor grows tender or pines away. On the contrary, it acknowledges itself to be unworthy of every good and every gift of God, and only worthy of a hell more horrible than the one which exists. Wisdom and maturity are established in the soul. As a result the soul becomes ordered and so strengthened that it can face death. It possesses God to the fullness of its capacity. And God even expands the soul so that it may hold all that he wishes to place in it. The soul then sees the One who is, and it sees that all else is nothing except insofar as it takes its being from him. In comparison, everything up until now seems as nothing to it—as indeed, all created reality. Nor are death, infirmity, honor, or dishonor of any concern to it. The soul is so satisfied and at rest that it desires nothing; it even loses the capacity to desire and to act effectively because it is bound to God. In this light it sees so well that God does everything with order and appropriateness that even in his absence, it does not pine. Likewise it becomes so conformed to God's will that even in his absence it is content with everything he does and entrusts itself totally to him.

Paul Lachance, trans., *Angela of Foligno: Complete Works*, The Classics of Western Spirituality (Mahwah, N.J.: Paulist Press, 1993), 223.

LOVE

CATHERINE OF GENOA

God illumines us with that love which has no need of us and which sustains us even though many of us, considering our inclination to evil, may rightfully be considered his enemies. Our sins, as long as we are in this world, do not ever make Him so wrathful that He ceases to do us good. Indeed, the more distance our sins put between us and God, the more insistent His call to us not to turn our backs on Him. He loves us and will not ever leave off doing us good. He does so in so many ways that the creature may well ask: Who am I that God has no concern but me?

God shows the creature that Pure Love in which He created it, the same love that brought into being the angels and Adam, a pure and intense love with which He wishes to be loved.

(In making the creature subject to Him, God assured that

man, given the excellence of his body and soul, might not consider himself God; that is why He gave man a sense of dependence.)

This love pointed the greater good yet for which man was created: the return, body and soul, of the creature to his celestial home.

After this, God had the creature realize the wretchedness of sin, against which there was no defense save the love of God. He also showed the creature in a short-lived vision the flaming love of Christ, from His incarnation to His ascension, His work in freeing us from eternal damnation, and how the soul of man was free and subject to God.

God also showed the creature how patiently His love waited, how He abhorred many sins; for had the soul died then and there it would have been perpetually damned.

Her soul, he showed her, had come close to death. He alone in the gentlest of ways had saved her, acting on her with such tender affection that she was virtually forced to do His will.

For God is terrible only in dealing with sin, since in His presence there cannot be the slightest stain. Sin and sin alone is the object of God's hatred, for it prevents His love from transforming us.

In this life, but not in its aftermath, that flaming love never ceases, no matter what the sins of man. That merciful love, Catherine saw, penetrates as deep as hell. Although man merits limitless pain in an infinite time, God's mercy puts a limit not to the time but to the suffering.

In this world, the rays of God's love, unbeknownst to man, encircle man all about, hungrily seeking to penetrate him. When barred, when the soul damns itself, it is almost as if that voice were to say, "Such is the love I bear this soul that I would never wish to leave it."

Once the soul is emptied of love, however, it becomes as evil as love is gentle. I say almost, for God still shows it some mercy.

Serge Hughes, trans., *Catherine of Genoa: Purgation and Purgatory, The Spiritual Dialogue,* The Classics of Western Spirituality (New York: Paulist Press, 1979), 108–9.

LOVE

CATHERINE OF GENOA

The creature is incapable of knowing anything but what God gives it from day to day. If it could know (beforehand) the successive degrees that God intends to give it, it would never be quieted.... When from time to time I would advert to the matter, it seemed to me that my love was complete; but later, as time went on and my sight grew clearer, I became aware that I had had many imperfections.... I did not recognize them at first, because God-Love was determined to achieve the whole only little by little, for the sake of preserving my physical life, and so as to keep my behaviour tolerable for those with whom I lived. For otherwise, with such other insight, so many excessive acts would ensue, as to make one insupportable to oneself and to others.... Every day I feel that the motes are being removed, which this Pure Love casts out (*cava fuori*). Man cannot see these imperfections; indeed, since, if he saw these motes, he could not bear the sight, God ever lets him see the work he has achieved, as though no imperfections remained in it. But all the time God does not cease from continuing to remove them.... From time to time, I feel that many instincts are being consumed within me, which before had appeared to be good and perfect; but when once they have been consumed, I understand that they were bad and imperfect.... These things are clearly visible in the mirror of truth, that is of Pure Love, where everything is seen crooked which before appeared straight....

This our self-will is so subtle and so deeply rooted within our own selves, and defends itself with so many reasons, that, when we cannot manage to carry it out in one way, we carry it out in another. We do our own wills under many covers (pretexts),—of charity, of necessity, of justice, of perfection. ...I saw this love to have so open and so pure an eye, its sight to be so subtle and its seeing so far-reaching, that I stood astounded....True love wills to stand naked, without any kind of cover, in heaven and on earth, since it has not anything shameful to conceal. . . .This naked love ever sees the truth; whilst self-love can neither see it nor believe in it. . . . Pure love loves God without any *for* (any further motive). . . .

I see every one to be capable of my tender Love. . . . Truth being, by its very nature, communicable to all, cannot be the exclusive property of any one. . . .

Pure Love loves God without why or wherefore (*perchè*). . . . Since Love took over the care of everything, I have not taken care of anything, nor have I been able to work with my intellect, memory and will, any more than if I had never had them. Indeed every day I feel myself more occupied in Him, and with greater fire. . . . I had given the keys of the house to Love, with ample permission to do all that was necessary, and determined to have no consideration for soul or body, but to see that, of all that the law of pure love required, there should not be wanting the slightest particle (*minimo chè*).And I stood so occupied in contemplating this work of Love, that if He had cast me, body and soul, into hell, hell itself would have appeared to me all love and consolation. . . .

God and Sin, however slight, cannot live peaceably side by side (*stare insieme*). Since some little thing that you may have in your eye does not let you see the sun, we can make a comparison between God and the sun, and then between intellectual vision and that of the bodily eye. . . . After considering things as they truly are, I find myself constrained to live without self. . . . Since the time when God has given the light to the soul, it can no more desire to operate by means of that part of itself which is ever staining all things and rendering turbid the clear waters of God's grace.The soul then offers and remits itself entirely to Him, so that it can no more operate except to the degree and in the manner willed by tender Love Himself; and henceforth it does not produce works except such as are pure, full and sincere; and these are the works that please God-Love.

Thomas Kepler, comp., *An Anthology of Devotional Literature* (Grand Rapids, Mich.: Baker Book House, 1977), 252–53.

LOVE

CATHERINE OF SIENA

[God says:] Do you know how I show myself within the soul who loves me in truth and follows the teaching of this gently loving Word? I show my strength in many ways, according to her desire, but there are three principle ways.

The first is my showing of my love and affection in the person of the Word, my Son, through his blood poured out in such burning love. This love is known in two manners. Ordinary people, those who live in ordinary love, know it when they see and experience my love in all the different blessings they receive from me. But it is known in a special manner by those who have been made my friends. Beyond the knowledge of ordinary love, these taste it and know it and experience it and feel it in their very souls.

Love's second showing is simply in souls themselves, when I show myself to them in loving affection. I do not play favorites but I do respect holy desire, and I show myself in souls in proportion to the perfection with which they seek me. Sometimes I show myself (this is still the second showing) by giving them the spirit of prophecy and letting them see into the future. This can take many forms, depending on what I see to be their need or that of others.

At other times—and this is the third showing—I will make them aware of the presence of my Truth, my only-begotten Son, and this in different ways, according to their hunger and their will. Sometimes they seek me in prayer, wanting to know my power, and I satisfy them by setting him before their mind's eye. Sometimes they seek me in the mercy of the Holy Spirit, and then my goodness lets them taste the fire of divine charity by which they conceive true and solid virtues grounded in pure charity for their neighbors.

Suzanne Noffke, trans., *Catherine of Siena: The Dialogue,* The Classics of Western Spirituality (New York: Paulist Press, 1980), 116.

LOVE

CATHERINE OF SIENA

[God says:] Since she has learned that she can be of no profit to me, nor return to me the same pure love with which she feels herself loved by me, she sets herself to repaying my love through the means I have established— her neighbors. They are the ones to whom you must be of service, just as I have told you that every virtue is realized through your neighbors. I have given you these to serve, every one, both in general and individually, according to the different graces you receive from me. You must love with the same pure love with which I loved you. But you cannot do this for me because I loved you without being loved and without any self-interest. And because I loved you without being loved by you, even before you existed (in fact it was love that moved me to create you in my own image and likeness) you cannot repay me. But you must give this love to other people, loving them without being loved by them. You must love them without any concern for your own spiritual or material profit, but only for the glory and praise of my name, because I love them. In this way you will fulfill the whole commandment of the Law, which is to love me above all things and your neighbor as your very self.

Suzanne Noffke, trans., *Catherine of Siena: The Dialogue,* The Classics of Western Spirituality (New York: Paulist Press, 1980), 165.

LOVE

GERTRUDE MORE

O my God, let me walk in the way of love which knoweth not how to seek self in anything whatsoever. Let this love wholly possess my soul and heart, which I beseech Thee, may live and move only in, and out of, a pure and sincere love to Thee. Oh! that thy pure love were so grounded and established in my heart that I might sigh and pant without ceasing after Thee, and be able in strength of this Thy love to live without all comfort and consolation, human or divine. O sight to be wished, desired, and longed for, because once to have seen Thee is to have learned all things! Nothing can bring us to this sight but love. But what love must it be? Not a sensible love only, a childish love, a love which seeketh itself more than the Beloved. No, it must be an ardent love, a pure love, a courageous love, a love of charity, a humble love, and a constant love, not worn out with labours, nor daunted with any difficulties. O Lord, give this love into my soul, that I may never more live nor breathe but out of a most pure love of Thee, my All and only Good. Let me love Thee for Thyself, and nothing else but in and for Thee. Let me love nothing instead of Thee, for to give all for love is a most sweet bargain.... Let Thy love work in me and by men, and let me love Thee as Thou wouldst be loved by me. I cannot tell how much love I would have of Thee, because I would love Thee beyond all that can be imagined or desired by me. Be Thou in this, as in all other things, my chooser for me, for Thou art my only choice, most dear to me. The more I shall love Thee, the more will my soul desire Thee, and desire to suffer for Thee.

Thomas Kepler, comp., *An Anthology of Devotional Literature* (Grand Rapids, Mich.: Baker Book House, 1977), 339.

LOVE

HADEWIJCH OF ANTWERP (BRABANT)

At the New Year
We hope for the new season,
Bringing new blossoms
And manifold new joys.
Who suffers on account of Love
Can now live happily,
For She will not escape him!
In Her richness and Her power
Always new and always gentle,
Always gracious in Her ways,
Love sweetens with a recompense
Each new pain as it comes.

How new to my eyes
Is he who serves new Love
With renewed fidelity,
As a novice should rightly do
As soon as Love reveals Herself to him.
Even if he had few friends
That would matter very little
As long as he clings to Love.
For Love offers new gifts:
An entirely new spirit
That renews itself in all,
And Her new touch.

At every moment Love is new
And is renewed each day,
Those who are renewed, She causes to be reborn
To a goodness which is ever new.
Alas, how can one remain old,
Renouncing Love's presence,
Old in sadness

And without gain?
For such a one has strayed from the new path
And the newness escapes him,
That newness of a new Love
In the essential love of new lovers.

Alas, where is new Love
With her renewed gifts?
For my distress brings me
Many new woes;
My senses abandon me
In the rage of Love;
The abyss into which She hurls me
Is deeper than the ocean,
For Her chasms ever deeper
Open my wound anew.
Never shall I be healed
Unless I find again all Her fresh newness.

But the wise, the old who have been renewed,
Who give themselves anew to Love,
Abandoning themselves to Her entirely,
These I call young and old.
They live in exalted mood
For they cling to Love,
Gazing upon Her ardently.
Their power in Love grows,
For they must be as novices
And, as old, lean upon Love
And be led where the Beloved wishes them,
Their spirit renewed by a new yearning.

Those who attend Love's new school,
With new love,
Following new Love's counsel
In honor of a new fidelity,
Seem to be wandering aimlessly,
And yet they are deeply engulfed

In Love's disfavor
While they are yearning for Her.
And then there comes new clarity,
With all new truth,
Bringing new revelation
Confided to me in secret.

Oh, how sweet are the tidings
Though they bring new vicissitudes
And many new sufferings;
Yet there is a new security,
For Love will amply repay us
With great new honors.
Love shall raise us up
To Love's highest council
Where newness shall be in plenitude
In renewed and glorious fruition.
"New Love is wholly mine!"
Ah, rare is this new favor!

Both new and newly reborn
Must distrust and condemn
All those who fear this [true] newness
And renew themselves with alien novelties.

Emilie Zum Brunn and Georgette Epiney-Burgard, *Women Mystics in Medieval Europe* (New York: Paragon House, 1989), 115–17.

LOVE

HADEWIJCH OF ANTWERP (BRABANT)

Later, one Easter Sunday, I had gone to God; and he embraced me in my interior senses and took me away in spirit. He brought me before the Countenance of the Holy Spirit, who possesses the Father and the Son in one Essence. And from the total Being of that Countenance I received all understanding, and thus I read all my judgments. A voice issuing from this Countenance resounded so fearfully that it made itself heard above everything. And it said to me: "Behold, ancient one, you have called me and sought me, what and who I, Love, am, myriads of years before the birth of man! See and receive my Spirit! With regard to all things, know what I, Love, am in them! And when you fully bring me yourself, as pure humanity in myself, through all the ways of perfect Love, you shall have fruition of me as the Love who I am. Until that day, you shall love what I, Love, am. And then you will be love, as I am Love. And you shall not live less than what I, Love, am, from that day until the death that will make you alive. In my unity, you have received me and I have received you. Go forth, and live what I am; and return bringing me full divinity, and have fruition of me as who I am."

Then I returned to myself, and I understood all I have just said; and I remained to gaze fixedly upon my delightful sweet Love.

Mother Columba Hart, trans., *Hadewijch: The Complete Works,* The Classics of Western Spirituality (New York: Paulist Press, 1980), 272.

LOVE

HADEWIJCH OF ANTWERP (BRABANT)

Time Is New With Every Year

Time is new with every year:
days of darkness become light.
Seeking love while lacking it,
oh, the wonder of such hope!

This new year is coming in!
For the man who turns his mind,
through some effort great or small
toward love, his grief is gain.

One who loves, yet spares the pain,
and so shows his lowliness,
wraps himself in stolen joys:
Rightly shall he feel their weight.

Those who come to life from love
and are nature's chosen ones
spare no toil for such a goal:
They will live in saintly warmth.

One who reaches love's high mount
he it is who welcomes pain,
for he looks upon his work
knowing well it has no end.

Shame upon the finer heart
which, by outer pressure duped,
fails to do the higher deed
that will keep its hunger keen.

Craving, sating—both in one—
such is the reward of love
as it may be seen by those
who consort in truth with it.

Craving: "Come, O Love supreme."
Sating: "Stop!" Such is the moan
for its light becomes too bright
and its blows turn into joy.

How can Love be deemed enough?
Oh, the marvel, it is he
who bestows his highest self
and imparts his treasured wealth.

How can hunger sustain love?
When a man knows he cannot
consummate what he desires,
this makes hunger stronger still.

How can light of love be pain?
When we cannot stand its gifts.
Nothing will compare with it
since it has no base in time.

Pleasures are but joust and strife
of true love by night and day,
since a man has nothing left
but his faith in this high love.

Holy Love I recommend
to all those who look for it.
For this goal, spare not your pains,
but conform your life with it.

Mother Columba Hart, trans., *Hadewijch: The Complete Works,* The Classics of Western Spirituality (New York: Paulist Press, 1980), 272.

LOVE

HADEWIJCH OF ANTWERP (BRABANT)

I would like to come close to true Love
if I could but attain to its core
—yet not one of those busy with things
will be able to join in my song.

Naked Love that will spare not a soul
in the treacherous passage of life
will be seen in its simplicity
at the time unessentials are crushed.

Let all those who surrender to Love
give up creatures and union with them:
Poor in spirit in the kingdom of earth,
they shall hold the new life as their due.

Nor is this to go traveling far,
nor to look for some bread or some good:
Poor in spirit, they give up chimeras
in the folds of a broad unity.

For a soul with no end or prelude,
with no form and no reason or sense,
with no model, no thought and no sign
has no circle to narrow it down.

In this madness of widening union
poor in spirit and living as one,
they will find in it nothing but leisure
that will give them eternal repose.

All of this may be said in few words,
but the passing is long, I know well,
for torments in great number befall
every soul that goes through to the end.

José De Vinck, *Revelations of Women Mystics: From Middle Ages to Modern Times* (New York: Alba House, 1985), 35-36.

LOVE

MARGARET EBNER

My tenderly beloved Jesus Christ gave me many delightful things in that same year ... in which is sweet delight about which He alone knows. Frequently when I began my Pater Noster my heart was captured by such a mysterious grace that I did not know what should come of it. Sometimes because of this I could not pray. Then I sat there in the delight of divine joy from matins until prime. Sometimes this was given to me so that within me arose the Speaking about which I have written before. Sometimes I was raised up so that I no longer touched the ground. Sometimes it was given to me to sit there in the wonderful joy of divine delight, unable to pray, but I could think about God and say whatever I wished. And with this it went well with me. Now He, from whom all grace flows, knows well what sort of graces there are, but to my human understanding these are incomprehensible. Also my Lord Jesus Christ knows well that I yearn for the dearest will of God all my life long. Whatever He gives me, I accept gladly. At all times, I desire to die in His love. Sometimes such great love for God takes hold of me that I cannot believe that God could ever have been so loved by another human being except by our tenderly beloved Lady and by His Beloved Disciple, St. John.

Leonard Hindsley, trans. and ed., *Margaret Ebner: Major Works,* The Classics of Western Spirituality (Mahwah, N.J.: Paulist Press, 1993), 111.

LOVE

MARGARET EBNER

On Friday after St. James' Day I went into choir and began my Pater Noster. Then the greatest grace overcame me and I knew not how it would end, except that I perceived the grace was so great that I could not finish the Pater Noster. My heart was surrounded by such sweet grace and felt so light that I was no longer able to pray. I held the Name Jesus Christus within me with sweet loving power and from it I perceived wonderful, sweet fragrances rising up within me.

Also, a wonderful desire was given me in the sweetness of grace especially to grasp the pure truth both from God and in God. At that time I had such a feeling and such an understanding of the presence of God and of the Truth, who is the Lord Himself, that if I possessed it all the time, it would be like heaven on earth. Also, in true love it was granted me to yearn for many great, mysterious desires. Then I was answered,

> I have given myself to you and will never withdraw myself from you. It is I alone, the true God who should possess your heart. All your delight is in me and all my delight is in your soul and in your heart. You are my love as I am your love. You do not understand that it is my pure love from which all this comes to you. Suffer me for the sake of my love, because I cannot do without your acceptance of it. It is I alone, the pure Truth, who lives in you and works through you, and I have surrounded you with my mercy. Rejoice that the true God lives in you and that my goodness will never forsake you in time or in eternity. I am your sweet delight on earth and you are my joy in heaven. Compelled by my very great love I have chosen you for myself in order to accomplish in you yet more for my eternal honor here and hereafter. It is I alone, your Lord and your God and your only Love, who accomplish great things in you.

Leonard Hindsley, trans. and ed., *Margaret Ebner: Major Works,* The Classics of Western Spirituality (Mahwah, N.J.: Paulist Press, 1993), 160-61.

LOVE

MECHTHILD OF MAGDEBURG

THE SOUL

Fish cannot drown in water,
birds cannot sink in the air,
gold cannot perish
in the refiner's fire.
This has God given to all creatures:
to foster and seek their own nature.
How then can I withstand mine?
I must to God—
my Father through nature,
my Brother through humanity,
my Bridegroom through love.
His am I forever.

Think ye that fire
must utterly slay my soul?
Nay! Love can both fiercely scorch
and tenderly cherish and console.
Therefore be not troubled.

GOD

When I shine, thou must reflect,
when I flow, thou must race;
when thou sighest, thou dost draw
my divine Heart unto thee;
when thou weepest for me,
I take thee in my arms;
but when thou lovest me,
then are we twain one—
for thus united, nothing can separate us:
rather, a blissful waiting lies between us.

THE SOUL

Then, O Lord, I will wait with hunger and thirst,
eagerness and delight until that joyful hour
when the chosen words shall flow
from thy divine lips—
words which can be heard of none
save that soul alone which cuts itself loose
from the world to listen
to the words of thy mouth.
Such a soul alone can receive the Fount of Love.

José De Vinck, *Revelations of Women Mystics: From Middle Ages to Modern Times* (New York: Alba House, 1985), 16-17.

LOVE

TERESA OF AVILA

[I have a] silly way in which I often speak to Him without meaning what I am saying; for it is love that speaks, and my soul is so far transported that I take no notice of the distance that separates it from God.

E. Allison Peers, trans. and ed., *The Life of Teresa of Jesus: The Autobiography of Teresa of Avila* (New York: Image Books/Doubleday, 1991), 20.

MARY

GERTRUDE THE GREAT OF HELFTA

It was the hour of prayer and, coming into the presence of God, she asked him what subject he would most like her to apply herself to during that hour. The Lord answered: "Keep close to my mother who is seated at my side, and strive to praise her." Then she devoutly hailed the Queen of heaven with the verse: "Paradise of pleasure . . . ," praising her for having been the most pleasant abode which God's inscrutable wisdom, to whom all creatures are known, chose as his dwelling from among all the delectable pleasures of his Father. She prayed that she might obtain for her own heart such attractive and varied virtues that God might be pleased to dwell there also. At that, the blessed Virgin seemed to bend down, as though to plant in the heart of the suppliant various flowers of virtue, such as the rose of charity, the lily of chastity, the violet of humility, the heliotrope of obedience, and others of the same sort, showing by this how eager she always is to hear the prayers of those who call upon her.

Then, as Gertrude hailed her again with the verse: "Rejoice, O you who guide our ways. . .," she praised her for having ordered, better than all other human beings, the whole household of her affections, ways, and senses, and all her other emotions, with such diligence that the Lord who dwelt within her could be given the most seemly service; for she never committed any fault, in thought, word or deed. Gertrude prayed that she too might obtain the same grace. At that, the Virgin Mother seemed to send her own affections in the form of noble damsels, commanding them to join themselves to those of the suppliant, and to strive to serve the Lord with them and make up for any shortcomings that might be found in their service. In this way our Lady let it be known how eager she is to aid those who call upon her.

After a little time had passed, Gertrude said to the Lord: "O my brother, since you were made man to make up for all human defects, now deign to make up to your blessed Mother for what may have been lacking in my praise of her." When he heard these words, the Son of God arose and most reverently went to kneel before his Mother; bowing his head, he saluted her most courteously and affectionately, so that she could not but be pleased with the homage of one whose imperfections were so abundantly made up for by her most beloved Son.

The following day, as she was praying in this way, the Virgin Mother appeared to her in the presence of the ever adorable Trinity, which appeared in the form of a fleur-de-lys, as it is usually shown, with three petals, one erect and two turning downward. Thus she was given to understand that the blessed Mother of God is justly called the White Lily of the Trinity, because she has received into herself, more fully and perfectly than any other creature, the virtues of the adorable Trinity; virtues which she never stained with even the least speck of venial sin. The erect petal denotes the omnipotence of God the Father; the two turning downward, the Wisdom and Love of the Son and the Holy Spirit, whom she most resembles. Wherefore she understood from the blessed Virgin that if one were to salute her devoutly with the words: "White Lily of the Trinity and fairest Rose of heavenly bliss," she would show how great is her power through the omnipotence of the Father; and with what ingenuity she knows how to work for the salvation of the human race, through the wisdom of the Son; and how immeasurably her heart bounds in tenderness, through the love of the Holy Spirit.

The blessed Virgin added: "Besides this, at the hour of death I shall appear to the soul who salutes me in this way in a blossoming of such beauty that she will be wondrously consoled as I reveal to her the bliss of heaven." From that time Gertrude resolved to salute the blessed Virgin, or her images, with these words: "Hail, white Lily of the resplendent and ever tranquil Trinity! Fairest Rose of heaven's bliss! The King of heaven chose to be born of you, to be fed with your milk! Oh, feed our souls on the outpourings of divine grace!"

Margaret Winkworth, trans. and ed., *Gertrude of Helfta: The Herald of Divine Love*, The Classics of Western Spirituality (Mahwah, N.J.: Paulist Press, 1993), 184–86.

MARY

HILDEGARD OF BINGEN

Mary,
ground of all being,
Greetings!

Greetings to you, lovely and loving Mother!
You birthed to earth your son,
You birthed the son of God from heaven
    by breathing the spirit of God.

Gabriele Uhlein, *Meditations with Hildegard of Bingen* (Santa Fe: Bear & Company, 1983), 115.

MARY

HILDEGARD OF BINGEN

They sang this song about holy Mary:

O most brilliant gem and serene glory of the sun,
you who the leaping fountain has been poured into
    from the heart of God,
the fountain is God's only Word
through which God created the first material of the
    world
which Eve threw into confusion;
God formed the Word—a person—from you,
and because of this you are that bright material
through which this very Word breathed out all the
    virtues,
just as God brought forth all the creatures from
    the first material.

O you, the sweetest virgin sprouting from the root
   of Jesse,
O how great is the virtue
which the divinity beheld in this most beautiful
   daughter,
as a water drop put into the divine eye—the sun,
when God directed the divine attention to the
   brightness of the Virgin
where God wishes the Word to be made flesh in her.

For by the mystical mystery of God, the bright
   flower went forth from this very Virgin, with
   the mind of the Virgin made wondrously light.

Bruce Hozeski, trans., *Hildegard von Bingen's Mystical Visions: Translated from Scivias,* introduced by Matthew Fox (Santa Fe: Bear & Company, 1995), 375-76.

NATURE

HILDEGARD OF BINGEN

The earth is at the same time
mother,
she is mother of all that is natural,
   mother of all that is human

She is the mother of all,
for contained in her
are the seeds of all.

The earth of humankind
contains all moistness,
   all verdancy,
   all germinating power.

It is in so many ways
fruitful.
All creation comes from it.

Yet it forms not only the basic
raw material for humankind,
but also the substance
of the incarnation
of God's son.

Flowing in and out like the breath,
the marrow of the hip sweats its essence,
carrying and strengthening the person.
In just such a manner
the vitality of earth's elements
comes from the strength of the creator.

It is this vigor that hugs the world:
warming, moistening, firming, greening.

This is so that all creatures
might germinate and grow.

Gabriele Uhlein, *Meditations with Hildegard of Bingen* (Santa Fe: Bear & Company, 1983), 58-59.

NATURE

MECHTHILD OF MAGDEBURG

God has granted to all creatures
That they live according to their nature.
How could I, then, oppose my nurture?
Far from all else, I must give myself to God
Who is my Father by nature,
My Brother through humanity,
My Betrothed in love.
And I, who am his without beginning,
Do you think I could not feel that nature? . . .
Spouse-soul, you must be so well "ennatured" in me
That nothing could exist between you and me.

José De Vinck, *Revelations of Women Mystics: From Middle Ages to Modern Times* (New York: Alba House, 1985), 8.

Night of the Soul

Teresa of Avila

I believe now that it was through the Lord's good providence that I found no one to teach me; for, had I done so, it would have been impossible, I think, for me to persevere during the eighteen years for which I had to bear this trial and *these great aridities, due, as I say, to my being unable to meditate.* During all these years, except after communicating, I never dared begin to pray without a book; my soul was as much afraid to engage in prayer without one as if it were having to go and fight against a host of enemies. With this help, which was a companionship to me and a shield with which I could parry the blows of my many thoughts, I felt comforted. For it was not usual with me to suffer from aridity: this only came when I had no book, whereupon my soul would at once become disturbed and my thoughts would begin to wander. As soon as I started to read they began to collect themselves and the book acted like a bait to my soul. Often the mere fact that I had it by me was sufficient. Sometimes I read a little, sometimes a great deal, according to the favour which the Lord showed me. It seemed to me, in these early stages of which I am speaking, that, provided I had books and could be alone, there was no risk of my being deprived of that great blessing.

E. Allison Peers, trans. and ed., *The Life of Teresa of Jesus: The Autobiography of Teresa of Avila* (New York: Image Books/Doubleday, 1991), 82.

PEACE

ANGELA OF FOLIGNO

To be transformed into Christ, the soul must imitate him in all the other virtues as well, such as peace and meekness

We should imitate our Lord Jesus Christ not only in those things just mentioned, but also in the other virtues. Peace is one, and we should be peaceful in words and deeds and in our way of life. But as to those defects and other things which threaten our soul, we should be like lions in expelling them. We should practice kindness and meekness not only among ourselves but with everyone in the measure fitting to each one. On the other hand, we should avoid too great a familiarity with the wicked, unless there is something in their behavior to call them to order on, and thus be of service to them. Let us, finally, be kind and meek, not returning evil with evil, but bearing it patiently.

Let us be indulgent toward those who offend us by word or deed, respond calmly, and not oppose them by taking note of the injury. It is with a calm exterior and a soul at rest that we must exercise indulgence to those who offend us, like a certain person would willingly kiss the feet of those who offend him. To acquire this virtue one should look at Christ and see how he bore offenses with kindness. His example gives us strength not to hold a grudge.

Finally, we should imitate Christ so as to remain straightforward in word and deed, without deception or duplicity.

Paul Lachance, trans., *Angela of Foligno: Complete Works,* The Classics of Western Spirituality (Mahwah, N.J.: Paulist Press, 1993), 289–90.

PEACE

HILDEGARD OF BINGEN

The other image, which was to her right, had the shape of an angel. She signifies peace. She springs forth from the greenness of truth because truth was surrounded with heavenly gifts at the time of the salvation of souls, a time of peace through the Word of God. What does this mean? The song of the angels once said: *Glory to God in the highest and peace on earth to men of good will (Luke 2:14).* This means that people shine in the highest God, and God shines in people since the Word of God was made flesh wondrously. Therefore, God in heaven is worthy of the praise and glory of every creature. And the peace of salvation may be on earth to those people who accept the will of God with devotion and faith, because the peace of a good will is also the will of God—who is complete goodness—and the will of the Word—who is both God and human.

Peace has the shape of an angel because she flees from every evil and beholds God with a holy intention—that is, in her own shape with angelic desire. This image had a wing upraised from each side. This means that she stretches upward to God both while tranquil and while agitated. She does not cause fear nor bitterness, but she always exists with peaceful prosperity. In other words, she understands the one God in the unity of her two wings. She is not confronted with any storm of unsteadiness regarding either good or evil, but she persists with a great deal of tranquility.

But this image appeared as a human otherwise. This means that peace shone wonderfully through the Word of God whose peacefulness made all the virtues good. Peace does not seek strife or a quarrel in any way, but always seeks gentleness. As a result, she is opposed to the devil, as she has shone in the words which she spoke earlier.

Bruce Hozeski, trans., *Hildegard von Bingen's Mystical Visions: Translated from Scivias,* introduced by Matthew Fox (Santa Fe: Bear & Company, 1995), 255.

PRAYER

ANGELA OF FOLIGNO

No one can be saved without divine light. Divine light causes us to begin and to make progress, and it leads us to the summit of perfection. Therefore if you want to begin and to receive this divine light, pray. If you have begun to make progress and want this light to be intensified within you, pray. And if you have reached the summit of perfection, and want to be superillumined so as to remain in that state, pray.

If you want faith, pray. If you want hope, pray. If you want charity, pray. If you want poverty, pray. If you want obedience, pray. If you want chastity, pray. If you want humility, pray. If you want meekness, pray. If you want fortitude, pray. If you want some virtue, pray.

And pray in this fashion, namely, always reading the Book of Life, that is, the life of the God-man Jesus Christ, whose life consisted of poverty, pain, contempt, and true obedience.

Paul Lachance, trans., *Angela of Foligno: Complete Works,* The Classics of Western Spirituality (Mahwah, N.J.: Paulist Press, 1993), 234.

PRAYER

ANGELA OF FOLIGNO

Once you have entered this way and are making progress in it, tribulations, temptations from demons, the world, and the flesh, will plague you in many ways and afflict you horribly; but if you want to overcome these, pray. And when the soul wants to improve its prayer, it must enter into it with a cleansed mind and body, and with pure and right intention. Its task is also to turn evil into good, and not, as many of the wicked do, convert good into evil. A soul thus exercised in cleansing itself goes with greater confidence to confession to have its sins washed away. And so that nothing impure may remain, it puts itself to a kind of scrutiny. It enters into prayer and examines the good and evil it has done. As it tries to determine the intentions behind the good things it has done, it discovers how in its fasts, prayers, tears, and all its other good deeds, it has behaved deceitfully, that is inadequately and defectively. You are not to behave, therefore, like the wicked, but rather confess your sins diligently and grieve over them for it is in confession that the soul is cleansed. After this, you are to return to prayer and not let yourself become preoccupied with anything else. As a result, you begin to feel the presence of God more fully than usual because your palate is more disposed to savor God's presence than before. It is through prayer, then, that one will be given the most powerful light to see God and self.

Paul Lachance, trans., *Angela of Foligno: Complete Works,* The Classics of Western Spirituality (Mahwah, N.J.: Paulist Press, 1993), 234.

PRAYER

ANGELA OF FOLIGNO

The purpose of prayer is nothing other than to manifest God and self. And this manifestation of God and self leads to a state of perfect and true humility. For this humility is attained when the soul sees God and self. It is in this profound state of humility, and from it, that divine grace deepens and grows in the soul. The more divine grace deepens humility in the soul, the more divine grace can grow in this depth of humility. The more divine grace grows, the deeper the soul is grounded, and the more it is settled in a state of true humility. Through perseverance in true prayer, divine light and grace increase, and these always make the soul grow deep in humility as it reads, as has been said, the life of Jesus Christ, God and man. I cannot conceive anything greater than the manifestation of God and self. But this discovery, that is, this manifestation of God and self, is the lot only of those legitimate sons of God who have devoted themselves to true prayer.

Those who possess the spirit of true prayer will have the Book of Life, that is, the life of Jesus Christ, God and man, set before them, and everything they could want, they will find there. Thus they will be filled with its blessed teaching—which does not puff anyone up—and will find there every doctrine they and others need. Hence if you wish to be superenlightened and taught, read this Book of Life. If you do not simply skim through it but rather let it penetrate you while reading it, you will be taught everything needed for yourself and for others, no matter what your state of life. Also, if you read it carefully and not casually, you will be so inflamed by divine fire that you will accept every tribulation as the greatest consolation. It will even make you see that you are most unworthy of these tribulations, and what is more, if success or human praise should come your way because of whatever quality God has placed in you, you will not become vain or put on airs because of it. By reading in the Book of Life, you will see and know that, in truth, the praise is not meant for you. Not boasting or feeling superior about anything but always remaining humble is one the signs by which one can detect that one is in the state of divine grace.

Paul Lachance, trans., *Angela of Foligno: Complete Works,* The Classics of Western Spirituality (Mahwah, N.J.: Paulist Press, 1993), 236.

PRAYER

ANGELA OF FOLIGNO

There are three kinds of prayer: bodily, mental, and supernatural. Divine wisdom is most orderly and it imposes its order on all things. Through its ineffable wisdom it has ordained that one does not attain mental prayer unless one has first passed through bodily prayer, and likewise, one does not attain supernatural prayer unless one has first passed through bodily and mental prayer. Divine wisdom also wills and has ordained that the canonical hour be said at the hours assigned for each one of them unless one is totally unable to do so because of some serious bodily ailment or because one is so absorbed in a state of mental or supernatural prayer and experiencing such joy in that state that one is totally speechless. Divine wisdom likewise teaches that when possible the hours should be said with the mind in a state of quiet and, as is fitting, with the body attentive and in a recollected state.

The more you pray the more you will be enlightened; and the more you are enlightened, the more deeply and exaltedly you will see the supreme Good and what this supreme Good consists of; the deeper and more perfect your vision, the more you will love; the more you love, the more you will delight in what you see; the more you find delight, the more you will understand and be made capable of understanding. Afterward, you will come to the fullness of light because you will understand that you cannot understand.

Paul Lachance, trans., *Angela of Foligno: Complete Works,* The Classics of Western Spirituality (Mahwah, N.J.: Paulist Press, 1993), 237.

PRAYER

ANGELA OF FOLIGNO

It is in prayer that one finds God. There are three schools, that is three types of prayer, without which one does not find God. These are bodily, mental, and supernatural.

Bodily prayer takes place with the sound of words and bodily movement such as genuflections. I never abandon this type of prayer. For sometimes when I want to devote myself to mental prayer, I am impeded by my laziness or by sleepiness. So I turn to bodily prayer, which leads to mental prayer. It should be done with attention. For instance, when you say the Our Father, you should weigh carefully what you are saying. Do not run through it, trying to complete a certain number of them, like little ladies doing piece work.

Prayer is mental when meditating on God so occupies the soul that one thinks of nothing but God. If some other thought comes to mind I no longer call such prayers mental. Such prayer curbs the tongue and renders one speechless. The mind is so totally filled with God's presence that it cannot think or speak about anything except about God and in God. From mental prayer, then, we move on to supernatural prayer.

I call prayer supernatural when God, bestowing this gift upon the soul and filling it with his presence, so elevates the soul that it is stretched, as it were, beyond its natural capacities. In this type of prayer, the soul understands more of God than would seem naturally possible. It knows that it cannot understand, and what it knows it cannot explain, because all that it sees and feels is beyond its own nature.

In these three schools of prayer you come to know who you are and who God is. From the fact that you know, you love. Loving, you desire to possess what you love. And this is the sign of true love: that the one who loves is transformed, not partially, but totally, into the Beloved. But because this transformation does not go on without interruption, the soul is seized by the desire to seek all the ways by which it can be transformed into the will of the Beloved, so it can return again to that vision. It seeks what was loved by the Beloved. God the Father provided a way for us to attain this transformation and this way is through the Beloved, that is, through God's own Son, whom he made the Son of poverty, suffering, contempt, and true obedience.

Paul Lachance, trans., *Angela of Foligno: Complete Works*, The Classics of Western Spirituality (Mahwah, N.J.: Paulist Press, 1993), 286–87.

PRAYER

CATHERINE OF SIENA

And loving, she seeks to pursue truth and clothe herself in it. But there is no way she can so savor and be enlightened by this truth as in continual humble prayer, grounded in the knowledge of herself and of God. For by such prayer the soul is united with God, following in the footsteps of Christ crucified, and through desire and affection and the union of love he makes of her another himself.

Suzanne Noffke, trans., *Catherine of Siena: The Dialogue,* The Classics of Western Spirituality (New York: Paulist Press, 1980), 25.

PRAYER

CATHERINE OF SIENA

The soul, once on her way, must cross over by way of the teaching of Christ crucified, truly loving virtue and hating vice. If she perseveres to the end she will come to the house of self-knowledge, where she shuts herself up in watching and continuous prayer, completely cut off from worldly company.

Why does she shut herself up? Through fear, because she knows how imperfect she is. And through her longing to attain a genuine and free love. She sees well that there is no other way to attain it, and so she waits with a lively faith for my coming, so that she may grow in grace.

How does one come to know lively faith? By persevering in virtue. You must never turn back for anything at all. You must not break away from holy prayer for any reason except obedience or charity. For so often during the time scheduled for prayer the devil comes with all sorts of struggles and annoyances—even more than when you are not at prayer. He does this to make you weary of holy prayer.

Often he will say, "This sort of prayer is worthless to you. You should not think about or pay attention to anything except vocal prayer." He makes it seem this way so that you will become weary and confused, and abandon the exercise of prayer. But prayer is a weapon with which you can defend yourself against every enemy. If you hold it with love's hand and the arm of free choice, this weapon, with the light of most holy faith, will be your defense.

Suzanne Noffke, trans., *Catherine of Siena: The Dialogue,* The Classics of Western Spirituality (New York: Paulist Press, 1980), 122.

PRAYER

JULIAN OF NORWICH

So our Lord wants us both to pray and to trust, for the reasons I have repeated were given to strengthen us against weakness in our prayers. For it is God's will that we pray, and he moves us to do so in these words I have told, for he wants us to be certain that our prayers are answered, because prayer pleases God. Prayers make a praying man pleased with him, and make the man serious and humble who before this was contending and striving against himself. Prayer unites the soul to God, for although the soul may always be like God in nature and substance, it is often unlike him in condition, through human sin. Prayer makes the soul like God when the soul wills as God wills; then it is like God in condition, as it is in nature. And so he teaches us to pray and to have firm trust that we shall have what we pray for, because everything which is done would be done, even though we had never prayed for it. But God's love is so great that he regards us as partners in his good work; and so he moves us to pray for what it pleases him to do, for whatever prayer or good desire comes to us by his gift he will repay us for, and give us eternal reward. And this was revealed to me when he said: If you beseech it.

In this saying God showed me his great pleasure and great delight, as though he were much beholden to us for each good deed that we do, even though it is he who does it. Therefore we pray much that he may do what is pleasing to him, as if he were to say: How could you please me more than by entreating me, wisely, sincerely, to do the thing that is my will? And so prayer makes harmony between God and man's soul, because when man is at ease with God he does not need to pray, but to contemplate reverently what God says. For in all the time when this was revealed to me, I was not moved to pray, but always to keep this good in my mind for my strength, that when we see God we have what we desire, and then we do not need to pray. But when we do not see God, then we need to pray, because we are failing, and for the strengthening of ourselves, to Jesus. For when a soul is tempted, troubled and left to itself in its unrest, that is the time for it to pray and to make itself simple and obedient to God. Unless the soul be obedient, no kind of prayer makes God supple to it; for God's love does not change, but during the time that a man is in sin he is so weak, so foolish, so unloving that he can love neither God nor himself.

Edmund Colledge and James Walsh, trans., *Julian of Norwich: Showings,* The Classics of Western Spirituality (New York: Paulist Press, 1978), 158–59.

PRAYER

JULIAN OF NORWICH

Jesus' words to her: "Pray inwardly, even if you feel no reward: it is profitable enough even if you feel nothing, see nothing, yes, even if it seems you can do nothing. In dryness and barrenness, in sickness and weakness, your prayer is most pleasing to me (though you seem to have little taste for it). And so it is in my sight with all your prayers of faith."

José De Vinck, *Revelations of Women Mystics: From Middle Ages to Modern Times* (New York: Alba House, 1985), 64.

PRAYER

MARGARET EBNER

This was also revealed to me in prayer: when I wish to pray for anything that weighs heavily upon my heart or upon the hearts of others, and it seems to me that it is necessary, but then I cannot put it into words except to say, "Lord accomplish your most loving will." He fulfills many of my dearest wishes; yes, I say truthfully that He never denies me one. He brings it about in truly divine joy.

Leonard Hindsley, trans. and ed., *Margaret Ebner: Major Works,* The Classics of Western Spirituality (Mahwah, N.J.: Paulist Press, 1993), 105.

PRAYER

TERESA OF AVILA

Not long ago a very learned man told me that souls who do not practice prayer are like people with paralyzed or crippled bodies; even though they have hands and feet they cannot give orders to these hands and feet. Thus there are souls so ill and so accustomed to being involved in external matters that there is no remedy, nor does it seem they can enter within themselves. They are now so used to dealing always with the insects and vermin that are in the wall surrounding the castle that they have become almost like them. And though they have so rich a nature and the power to converse with none other than God, there is no remedy. If these souls do not strive to understand and cure their great misery, they will be changed into statues of salt, unable to turn their heads to look at themselves, just as Lot's wife was changed for having turned her head.

Insofar as I can understand, the gate of entry to this castle is prayer and reflection. I don't mean to refer to mental more than vocal prayer, for since vocal prayer is prayer it must be accompanied by reflection. A prayer in which a person is not aware of whom he is speaking to, what he is asking, who it is who is asking and of whom, I do not call prayer however much the lips may move. Sometimes it will be so without this reflection, provided that the soul has these reflections at other times. Nonetheless, anyone who has the habit of speaking before God's majesty as though he were speaking to a slave, without being careful to see how he is speaking, but saying whatever comes to his head and whatever he has learned from saying at other times, in my opinion is not praying. Please God, may no Christian pray in this way. Among yourselves, Sisters, I hope in His Majesty that you will not do so, for the custom you have of being occupied with interior things is quite a good safeguard against falling and carrying on in this way like brute beasts.

Kieran Kavanaugh and Otilio Rodriguez, trans., *Teresa of Avila: The Interior Castle*, The Classics of Western Spirituality (New York: Paulist Press, 1979), 38.

PRAYER

TERESA OF AVILA

On the way there, I stopped at the house of this uncle of mine, which, as I have said, was on the road, and he gave me a book called *Third Alphabet*, which treats of the *Prayer of Recollection*. During this first year I had been reading good books (I no longer wanted to read any others, for I now realized what harm they had done me) but I did not know how to practise prayer, or how to recollect myself, and so I was delighted with the book and determined to follow that way of prayer with all my might. As by now the Lord had granted me the gift of tears, and I liked reading, I began to spend periods in solitude, to go frequently to confession and to start upon the ways of prayer with this book for my guide. For I found no other guide (no confessor, I mean) who understood me, though I sought one for fully twenty years subsequently to the time I am speaking of. This did me great harm, as I had frequent relapses, and might have been completely lost; a guide would at least have helped me to escape when I found myself running the risk of offending God.

E. Allison Peers, trans. and ed., *The Life of Teresa of Jesus: The Autobiography of Teresa of Avila* (New York: Image Books/Doubleday, 1991), 80–82.

SACRAMENT

CATHERINE OF SIENA

[God says:] It is with this love that you come to receive my gracious glorious light, the light I have given you as food, to be administered to you by my ministers. But even though all of you receive the light, each of you receives it in proportion to the love and burning desire you bring with you. It is just like the example I gave you of the people whose candles received the flame according to their weight. Each of you carries the light whole and undivided, for it cannot be divided by any imperfection in you who receive it or in those who administer it. You share as much of the light (that is, the grace you receive in this sacrament) as your holy desire disposes you to receive.

But anyone who would approach this gracious sacrament while guilty of deadly sin would receive no grace from it, even though such a person would really be receiving me as I am, wholly God, wholly human. But do you know the situation of the soul who receives the sacrament unworthily? She is like a candle that has been doused with water and only hisses when it is brought near the fire. The flame no more than touches it but it goes out and nothing remains but smoke. Just so, this soul brings the candle she received in holy baptism and throws the water of sin over it, a water that drenches the wick of baptismal grace that is meant to bear the light. And unless she dries the wick out with the fire of true contrition by confessing her sin, she will physically receive the light when she approaches the table of the altar, but she will not receive it into her spirit.

Suzanne Noffke, trans., *Catherine of Siena: The Dialogue,* The Classics of Western Spirituality (New York: Paulist Press, 1980), 208–12.

SACRAMENT

CATHERINE OF SIENA

[God says:] If the soul is not disposed as she should be for so great a mystery, this true light will not graciously remain in her but will depart, leaving her more confounded, more darksome, and more deeply in sin. She will have gained nothing from this sacrament but the hissing of remorse, not because of any defect in the light (for nothing can impair it) but because of the water it encountered in the soul, the water that so drenched her love that she could not receive the light.

So you see, in no way can the heat and color and brightness that are fused in this light be divided—not by the scant desire the soul brings to this sacrament, nor by any fault in the soul who receives it or in the one who administers it. It is like the sun, which is not contaminated by the filth it shines on. Nothing can contaminate or divide the gentle light in this sacrament. Its brightness is never diminished and it never strays from its orbit, though the whole world shares in the light and heat of this Sun. So this Word, this Sun, my only-begotten Son, never strays from me, the eternal Sun and Father. In the mystic body of holy Church he is administered to everyone who will receive him. He remains wholly with me and wholly you have him, God and human, just as I told you in the example of the lamp. Though all the world should ask for his light, all would have it whole, and whole it would remain.

Suzanne Noffke, trans., *Catherine of Siena: The Dialogue,* The Classics of Western Spirituality (New York: Paulist Press, 1980), 208–9.

SACRAMENT

CATHERINE OF SIENA

[God says:] O dearest daughter, open wide your mind's eye and look into the abyss of my charity. There is not a person whose heart would not melt in love to see, among all the other blessings I have given you, the blessing you receive in this sacrament.

And how, dearest daughter, should you and others look upon this mystery and touch it? Not only with your bodily eyes and feeling, for here they would fail you. You know that all your eyes see is this white bit of bread; this is all your hand can touch and all your tongue can taste, so that your dull bodily senses are deceived. But the soul's sensitivity cannot be deceived, unless she so chooses by extinguishing the light of holy faith by infidelity.

What tastes and sees and touches this sacrament? The soul's sensitivity. How does she see it? With her mind's eye, so long as it has the pupil of holy faith. This eye sees in that whiteness the divine nature joined with the human; wholly God, wholly human; the body, soul, and blood of Christ, his soul united with his body and his body and soul united with my divine nature, never straying from me. This, if you remember, is what I revealed to you early in your life and that not only to your mind's eye but to your bodily eyes as well, although because of the great light you soon lost your bodily sight and were left with only your spiritual vision.

Suzanne Noffke, trans., *Catherine of Siena: The Dialogue,* The Classics of Western Spirituality (New York: Paulist Press, 1980), 209-10.

Sacrament

Catherine of Siena

[God says:] How is this sacrament touched? With the hand of love. This hand it is that touches what the eye has seen and known in this sacrament. The hand of love touches through faith, confirming as it were what the soul sees and knows spiritually through faith.

How is this sacrament tasted? With holy desire. The body tastes only the flavor of bread, but the soul tastes me, God and human. So you see, the body's senses can be deceived, but not the soul's. In fact, they confirm and clarify the matter for her, for what her mind's eye has seen and known through the pupil of holy faith, she touches with the hand of love. What she has seen she touches in love and faith. And she tastes it with her spiritual sense of holy desire, that is, she tastes the burning, unspeakable charity with which I have made her worthy to receive the tremendous mystery of this sacrament and its grace.

So you see, you must receive this sacrament not only with your bodily senses but with your spiritual sensitivity, by disposing your soul to see and receive and taste this sacrament with affectionate love.

Dearest daughter, contemplate the marvelous state of the soul who receives this bread of life, this food of angels, as she ought. When she receives this sacrament she lives in me and I in her. Just as the fish is in the sea and the sea in the fish, so am I in the soul and the soul in me, the sea of peace. Grace lives in such a soul because, having received this bread of life in grace, she lives in grace. When this appearance of bread has been consumed, I leave behind the imprint of my grace, just as a seal that is pressed into warm wax leaves its imprint when it is lifted off. Thus does the power of this sacrament remain there in the soul; that is, the warmth of my divine charity, the mercy of the Holy Spirit, remains there. The light of my only-begotten Son's wisdom remains there, enlightening the mind's eye. [The soul] is left strong, sharing in my strength and power, which make her strong and powerful against her selfish sensuality and against the devil and the world.

So you see, the imprint remains once the seal is lifted off. In other words, once the material appearances of the bread have been consumed, this true Sun returns to his orbit. Not that he had ever left it, for he is united with me. But my deep charity gave him to you as food for your salvation and for your nourishment in this life where you are pilgrim travelers, so that you would have refreshment and would not forget the blessing of the blood. I in my divine providence gave you this food, my gentle Truth, to help you in your need.

See, then, how bound and obligated you are to love me in return, since I have loved you so much, and because I am supreme eternal Goodness, deserving to be loved by you.

Suzanne Noffke, trans., *Catherine of Siena: The Dialogue,* The Classics of Western Spirituality (New York: Paulist Press, 1980), 211.

SACRAMENT

CATHERINE OF SIENA

[God says:] Do you know, dearest daughter, how I provide for these servants of mine who put their trust in me? In two ways, for all my providence for my rational creatures is for both soul and body. And whatever I do to provide for the body is done for the good of the soul, to make her grow in the light of faith, to make her trust in me and give up trusting in herself, and to make her see and know that I am who I am and that I can and will and know how to assist her in her need and save her.

I have given the soul the sacraments of holy Church for her life, to be her food. Heavy physical bread is given as food for the body. But because the soul is incorporeal, she lives by my word. Thus my Truth in the holy Gospel said that people do not live by bread alone, but by every word that comes from me, that is, by following with spiritual understanding the teaching of my incarnate Word. This Word and the holy sacraments give you life in virtue of the blood. So you see, spiritual sacraments are given to the soul. Although they are performed and given by means of the body, that act of itself would not give the soul the life of grace unless the soul received it with the disposition of true holy spiritual desire. And this desire is in the soul, not in the body. This is why I told you that the sacraments are spiritual and are given to the soul because the soul is incorporeal. And though they are carried by means of the body it is the soul that receives them.

Sometimes, to intensify her hunger and holy desire, I will let her desire them when she cannot have them. Because she cannot have them her hunger grows, and with her hunger her self-knowledge grows because in her humility she considers herself unworthy. Then I make her worthy, and often I provide this sacrament in different ways.

Suzanne Noffke, trans., *Catherine of Siena: The Dialogue,* The Classics of Western Spirituality (New York: Paulist Press, 1980), 293.

SERVICE

ANGELA OF FOLIGNO

"I who speak to you am the divine Might who bring you a favor. This is the favor I am bringing you: I want you to be useful to all who will see you. Even more: I want you also to help and be useful to all who think of you and who hear your name. The more someone will possess me, the more useful shall you be to him."

José De Vinck, *Revelations of Women Mystics: From Middle Ages to Modern Times* (New York: Alba House, 1985), 55.

Silence

Margaret Ebner

Silence suits me so well and I have such great grace and peace from it that I practice it in Lent and throughout the year and am greatly annoyed with others when I have to speak. I am so content with this inner peace that I cannot suffer external speech, especially after Easter. My Truth, Jesus Christ, knows well that my soul heartily loves and holds dear this silence and solitude because I have perceived great grace from them.

Leonard Hindsley, trans. and ed., *Margaret Ebner: Major Works,* The Classics of Western Spirituality (Mahwah, N.J.: Paulist Press, 1993), 109.

Sin

Julian of Norwich

Sin has to happen, but all shall be well. All shall be well, and all manner of things shall be well.

Through this naked word, "sin," the Lord brought to my mind everything in general that is not good: the shameful contempt and utter annihilation he suffered for us in this life; his dying and all the spiritual and bodily pains of his creatures. For all of us are, at least in part, reduced to nothing, and shall so be reduced, following our Master Jesus, until we are fully cleansed, that is, until we are fully stripped of our mortal flesh and of all those inner affections of ours that are not really good. . . .

Because of the tender love our Lord has for all those who are to be saved, he comforts them swiftly and sweetly, saying "It is true that sin is the cause of all this pain, but all shall be well. All shall be well, and all manner of things shall be well."

These words were said most tenderly, without implying any blame to me or to anyone else of future elect. . . .

In these same words, I saw a marvelous high secret hidden in God—to be made known to us openly in heaven. By knowing it, we shall truly see why he allowed sin to come, and in this sight, we shall rejoice forever in our Lord God.

José De Vinck, *Revelations of Women Mystics: From Middle Ages to Modern Times* (New York: Alba House, 1985), 69–70.

SOUL

MARGUERITE PORETE

Reason: Ah, Love, says Reason, name this Soul by her right name, give to the Actives some understanding of it.

Love: She can be named, says Love, by twelve names; that is:

The very marvelous one.
The Not Understood.
Most Innocent of the Daughters of Jerusalem.
She upon whom the Holy Church is founded.
Illuminated by Understanding.
Adorned by Love.
Living by Praise.
Annihilated in all things through Humility.
At peace in divine being through divine will.
She who wills nothing except the divine will.
Filled and satisfied without any lack by divine
    goodness through the work of the Trinity.
Her last name is: Oblivion, Forgotten.

These twelve names Love gives to her.

Pure Courtesy: And without fail, says Pure Courtesy, it is right that she be thus named, for these are her right names.

Reason: Ah, Love, you have named this Soul by many names, by which the Actives have some understanding of her, which would only be by hearing the very noble names by which you have named her.

Ellen L. Babinsky, trans., *Marguerite Porete: The Mirror of Simple Souls,* The Classics of Western Spirituality (Mahwah, N.J.: Paulist Press, 1993), 87–88.

SOUL

MECHTHILD OF MAGDEBURG

The true greeting of God, which comes from the heavenly flood out of the spring of the flowing Trinity, has such power that it takes all strength from the body and lays the soul bare to itself. Thus it sees itself as one of the blessed and receives in itself divine glory. The soul is then separated from the body, with its power and love and longing. Only the smallest part of life remains to the body, which is as it were in a sweet sleep. The soul sees God as One and Undivided in Three Persons, and the Three Persons in One Undivided God. God greets the soul in the language of the court of heaven not understood in this kitchen (the earthly world). And he clothes it with such garments as are worn in his palace and girds it with strength. Then it may ask what it will, and that shall be granted.

Should it not be granted, it is because the soul is taken further by God to a secret place where it must not ask nor pray for anyone, for God alone will play with it in a game of which the body knows nothing, any more than the peasant at the plough or the knight in the tourney—not even his loving Mother Mary: she can do nothing here. Thus God and the soul soar further to a blissful place of which I neither can nor will say much: it is too great and I dare not speak of it, for I am a sinful creature.

Moreover, when the infinite God brings the unmoored soul up into the heights of contemplation, it loses touch with the earth in face of that wonder, and forgets it ever was upon the earth. When this flight is at its height, the soul must leave it. Then the All-Glorious God speaks: "Maiden! thou must humble thyself and descend again."

She is affrighted, and says: "Lord! thou hast drawn me up so high that I am out of myself and cannot praise thee with any order in my body, for I suffer grievously and strive against my body."

Then he speaks: "Ah! my dove! thy voice is music to my ears, thy words are as savor to my mouth, thy longing as the gentleness of my gifts."
And she replies: "Dear Lord! all must be as the Master ordains."
And she sighs so deeply that her body is awakened and asks: "Lady, where hast thou been? Thou comest so lovingly back, so beautiful and strong, so free and full of spirit! But thy wanderings have taken from me my zest, my peace, my color, all my powers."
The soul exclaims: "Silence! Destroyer! Cease thy complaints! I will ever guard myself against thee. That my enemy should be wounded does not trouble me, I am glad of it."

José De Vinck, *Revelations of Women Mystics: From Middle Ages to Modern Times* (New York: Alba House, 1985), 10-12.

SPIRITUAL GIFTS

ANGELA OF FOLIGNO

Whoever has been able to obtain these most sweet gifts of God should know that he has reached consummation and perfection in the most sweet Lord Jesus Christ; and, likewise, has become this same most sweet Lord Jesus Christ through transformation. The more one grows in these gifts the more the being of the most sweet Jesus will grow in him.

The first gift is the love of poverty by which the soul strips itself of the love of every creature; does not want to possess anything other than our Lord Jesus Christ; does not place its hope in the help of any creature in this life; and shows this by its deeds.

The second gift is the desire to be despised, vilified, and covered with opprobrium by every creature. The soul wants everyone to believe that it is worthy of such treatment, so that it receives no sympathy from anyone. It wants to live in the heart of none except God, and receive no esteem whatsoever from anyone.

The third gift is the desire to be afflicted, burdened, filled, submerged, with all the sufferings of the body and heart which the most sweet Lord Jesus and his most sweet mother endured. Furthermore, with this gift the soul wants every creature to inflict these sufferings on it without intermission. If you cannot want these three—poverty, suffering, and contempt—you should know that you are far from resembling the blessed and most sweet Christ. For poverty, suffering, and contempt accompanied him in the highest degree, everywhere, all the time, and in everything that he did. They likewise accompanied his mother in the highest degree.

The fourth gift is that you know you are unworthy of receiving such a great benefit and, likewise, totally incapable, by yourself, of possessing these—that is, poverty, suffering, and contempt. For when you presume too much that you possess the one you love, you lose love. Therefore you never feel that you have succeeded in attaining this gift, but it seems to you that you are always just starting anew, that you have never done anything until now, and that you have never had any of these three.

Paul Lachance, trans., *Angela of Foligno: Complete Works,* The Classics of Western Spirituality (Mahwah, N.J.: Paulist Press, 1993), 285–86.

Spiritual Gifts

Angela of Foligno

The fifth gift is to constantly strive to think how these three [poverty, suffering, and contempt] existed in the Lord Jesus Christ and, in continual longing prayer, to cry out to the Lord that he might give you these three that were garments, his companions, and send them deep into your heart, and not to ask anything for yourself. It is this perfect transformation into poverty, suffering, and contempt that you should place all your joy in this life. You should strive to lift yourself to the level of imagining how the heart of the most sweet Jesus was filled and overflowed with all these three, infinitely more than what was visible in his body. The sixth gift is to flee like the worst pestilence all those, be they spiritual or carnal persons, who impede the soul from acquiring these three; and, likewise, to hold in horror, despise, and flee, as if it were a serpent, all that in this life seems to be different from or opposed to these three.

The seventh gift is not to pass judgment on any creature, nor to get bogged down trying to judge others, as the gospel says, but rather to esteem yourself as more vile than the others, no matter how wicked, and as unworthy of any grace from God.

Because the soul is still weak and cannot yet serve God without the hope of a reward, it is given to know that these gifts merit possessing God fully in the heavenly homeland, or rather, that the soul, through the transformation realized by these gifts, becomes God totally. This is true to such an extent that even in this life God bestows a great deal of this full transformation to souls who are thus transformed into his contempt, poverty, and suffering. The soul, however, should not seek and desire in this life the consolations that accompany these gifts, unless perhaps when, in its weakness, it needs strengthening. The soul's one desire should be to attain the perfect crucifixion of Christ, his suffering, poverty, and contempt.

Paul Lachance, trans., *Angela of Foligno: Complete Works,* The Classics of Western Spirituality (Mahwah, N.J.: Paulist Press, 1993), 285–86.

SUFFERING

CATHERINE OF SIENA

[God says:] So you see, suffering atones for sin not by reason of the finite pain but by reason of perfect contrition of the heart. And in those who have this perfect contrition it atones not only for the sin itself but for the penalty due that sin. But for most, as I have said, their suffering satisfies only for sin itself; for though they are freed from deadly sin and receive grace, if their contrition and love are not strong enough to satisfy for the penalty, they go to the pains of purgatory once they have passed beyond the second and final means.

The willing desire to suffer every pain and hardship even to the point of death for the salvation of souls is very pleasing to me. The more you bear, the more you show your love for me. In loving me you come to know more of my truth, and the more you know, the more intolerable pain and sorrow you will feel when I am offended.

You asked for suffering, and you asked me to punish you for the sins of others. What you were not aware of was that you were, in effect, asking for love and light and knowledge of the truth. For I have already told you that suffering and sorrow increase in proportion to love: When love grows, so does sorrow. So I say to you: Ask and it shall be given to you; I will not say no to anyone who asks in truth. Consider that the soul's love in divine charity is so joined with perfect patience that the one cannot leave without the other. The soul, therefore, who chooses to love me must also choose to suffer for me anything at all that I give her. Patience is not proved except in suffering, and patience is one with charity, as has been said. Endure courageously, then. Otherwise you will not show yourselves to be—nor will you be—faithful spouses and children of my Truth, nor will you show that your delight is in my honor and in the salvation of souls.

Suzanne Noffke, trans., *Catherine of Siena: The Dialogue*, The Classics of Western Spirituality (New York: Paulist Press, 1980), 32–33.

Suffering

Catherine of Siena

[God says:] Let every soul rejoice who suffers many troubles, because such is the road that leads to this delightfully glorious state. I have told you before that you reach perfection through knowledge and contempt of yourself and knowledge of my goodness. And at no time does the soul know herself so well, if I am within her, as when she is most beleaguered. Why? I will tell you. She knows herself well when she finds herself besieged and can neither free herself nor resist being captured. Yes, she can resist with her will to the point of not giving her consent, but that is all. Then she can come to know that [of herself] she is nothing. For if she were anything at all of herself, she would be able to get rid of what she did not want. So in this way she is humbled in true self-knowledge, and in the light of holy faith she runs to me, God eternal. For by my kindness she was able to maintain her good and holy will steadfast when she was sorely besieged, so that she did not imitate the wretched things that were vexing her.

You have good reason, then, to take comfort in the teaching of the gentle loving Word, my only-begotten Son, in times of great trouble, suffering and adversity, and when you are tempted by people or the devil. For these things strengthen your virtue and bring you to great perfection.

Suzanne Noffke, trans., *Catherine of Siena: The Dialogue,* The Classics of Western Spirituality (New York: Paulist Press, 1980), 168.

Suffering

Margaret Ebner

When I heard that someone was angry with our serving girls and had said to them, "You are not worthy to serve us," heartfelt sorrow overcame me so that I cried and thought, "God has never said that I was unworthy to serve Him." I could not bear the slaughtering of the cattle and when I saw that they were being slaughtered I began to cry and thought that God had never slaughtered me because of my misdeeds. I had compassion for all things and true compassion for everyone whom I saw suffering, no matter what kind of suffering it was. With God's help I have avoided afflicting anyone or being harsh with anyone, and also I myself was never afflicted by anyone.

Leonard Hindsley, trans. and ed., *Margaret Ebner: Major Works,* The Classics of Western Spirituality (Mahwah, N.J.: Paulist Press, 1993), 90.

Suffering

Margaret Ebner

In his goodness God preserved me from becoming depressed or impatient out of misery or sorrow. Whatever anyone did for me I considered it good and whatever was not done for me I tried to endure also for God's sake. I spent almost the whole of Lent in great pain. After Easter I regained my health so that I could follow the nuns into choir and everywhere else with delight and joy. The sorrow for my sister was so diminished that I was able to give her over to God gladly. I began to experience more vividly the grace of God inwardly and outwardly. Especially when I came to my Lord with a grievous concern standing before the altar in the choir, it was taken away from me by the grace of God. It seemed to me that I was like someone who carries a heavy burden and lays it down. I was troubled when our monastery was not doing well in spiritual and material matters or when I saw that someone acted contrary to truth or peace or love or when someone rejoiced over the bad fortune of another or other such things. I suffered the greatest sorrow from this, and it gave me so much pain that I often went away crying. I treated this pain as a gift sent to me by God so that I would recognize that I myself did not yet live according to peace, truth, and love as I should.

Leonard Hindsley, trans. and ed., *Margaret Ebner: Major Works*, The Classics of Western Spirituality (Mahwah, N.J.: Paulist Press, 1993), 94.

TEMPTATION

CATHERINE OF SIENA

[God says:] No one need fear any battle or temptation of the devil that may come, for I have made you strong and given your wills power in the blood of my Son. Neither the devil nor any other creature can change this will of yours, for it is yours, given by me with the power of free choice. You, then, can hold or loose it as you please, by your free choice. It is a weapon that, as soon as you put it in the devil's hands, becomes a knife with which he pursues and kills you. But if you refuse to put this weapon, your will, into the devil's hands (that is, if you refuse to consent to his tempting and troubling) you will never be hurt in any temptation by the guilt of sin. Indeed, temptation will strengthen you, provided you open your mind's eye to see my charity, which lets you be tempted only to bring you to virtue and to prove your virtue.

You cannot arrive at virtue except through knowing yourself and knowing me. And this knowledge is more perfectly gained in time of temptation, because then you know that you are nothing, since you have no power to relieve yourself of the sufferings and troubles you would like to escape. And you know me in your will, when I strengthen it in my goodness so that it does not consent to these thoughts. You realize that my love has granted them, for the devil is weak and can do nothing of himself, but only as I permit him. And I give him leave not through hatred but through love, not so that you may be conquered but that you may conquer and come to perfect knowledge of yourself and of me, and to prove your virtue—for virtue can only be tested by its opposite.

Suzanne Noffke, trans., *Catherine of Siena: The Dialogue*, The Classics of Western Spirituality (New York: Paulist Press, 1980), 88.

TRINITY

CATHERINE OF SIENA

O eternal Trinity! O Godhead! That Godhead, your divine nature, gave the price of your Son's blood its value. You, eternal Trinity, are a deep sea: The more I enter you, the more I discover, and the more I discover, the more I seek you. You are insatiable, you in whose depth the soul is sated yet remains always hungry for you, thirsty for you, eternal Trinity, longing to see you with the light in your light. Just as the deer longs for the fountain of living water, so does my soul long to escape from the prison of my darksome body and see you in truth. O how long will you hide your face from my eyes?

O eternal Trinity, fire and abyss of charity, dissolve this very day the cloud of my body! I am driven to desire, in the knowledge of yourself that you have given me in your truth, to leave behind the weight of this body of mine and give my life for the glory and praise of your name. For by the light of understanding within your light I have tasted and seen your depth, eternal Trinity, and the beauty of your creation. Then, when I considered myself in you, I saw that I am your image. You have gifted me with power from yourself, eternal Father, and my understanding with your wis-

dom—such wisdom as is proper to your only-begotten Son;
and the Holy Spirit, who proceeds from you and from your
Son, has given me a will, and so I am able to love.

Suzanne Noffke, trans., *Catherine of Siena: The Dialogue,* The Classics of Western Spirituality (New York: Paulist Press, 1980), 364-65.

TRINITY

CATHERINE OF SIENA

You, eternal Trinity, are the craftsman; and I your handiwork have come to know that you are in love with the beauty of what you have made, since you made of me a new creation in the blood of your Son.

O abyss! O eternal Godhead! O deep sea! What more could you have given me than the gift of your very self?

You are a fire always burning but never consuming; you are a fire consuming in your heat all the soul's selfish love; you are a fire lifting all chill and giving light. In your light you have made me know your truth: You are that light beyond all light who gives the mind's eye supernatural light in such fullness and perfection that you bring clarity even to the light of faith. In that faith I see that my soul has life, and in that light receives you who are Light.

In the light of faith I gain wisdom in the wisdom of the Word your Son; in the light of faith I am strong, constant, persevering; in the light of faith I have hope: It does not let me faint along the way. This light teaches me the way, and without this light I would be walking in the dark. This is why I asked you, eternal Father, to enlighten me with the light of most holy faith.

Truly this light is a sea, for it nourishes the soul in you, peaceful sea, eternal Trinity. Its water is not sluggish; so the soul is not afraid because she knows the truth. It distills, revealing hidden things, so that here, where the most abundant light of your faith abounds, the soul has, as it were, a guarantee of what she believes. This water is a mirror in which you, eternal Trinity, grant me knowledge; for when I look into this mirror, holding it in the hand of love, it shows me myself, as your creation, in you, and you in me through the union you have brought about of the Godhead with our humanity. This light shows you to me, and in this light I know you, highest and infinite Good: Good above every good, joyous Good, Good beyond measure and understanding! Beauty above all beauty; Wisdom above all wisdom—indeed you are wisdom itself! You who are the angels' food are given to humans with burning love. You, garment who cover all nakedness, pasture the starving within your sweetness, for you are sweet without trace of bitterness.

Suzanne Noffke, trans., *Catherine of Siena: The Dialogue,* The Classics of Western Spirituality (New York: Paulist Press, 1980), 365-66.

TRINITY

CATHERINE OF SIENA

O eternal Trinity, when I received with the light of most holy faith your light that you gave me, I came to know therein the way of great perfection, made smooth for me by so many wonderful explanations. Thus I may serve you in the light, not in the dark; and I may be a mirror of a good and holy life; and I may rouse myself from my wretched life in which, always through my own fault, I have served you in darkness. I did not know your truth, and so I did not love it. Why did I not know you? Because I did not see you with the glorious light of most holy faith, since the cloud of selfish love darkened the eye of my understanding. Then with your light, eternal Trinity, you dispelled the darkness.

But who could reach to your height to thank you for so immeasurable a gift, for such generous favors, for the teaching of truth that you have given me? A special grace, this, beyond the common grace you give to other creatures. You willed to bend down to my need and that of others who might see themselves mirrored here.

You responded, Lord; you yourself have given and you yourself answered and satisfied me by flooding me with a gracious light, so that with that light I may return thanks to you. Clothe, clothe me with yourself, eternal Truth, so that I may run the course of this mortal life in true obedience and in the light of most holy faith. With that light I sense my soul once again becoming drunk! Thanks be to God! Amen.

Suzanne Noffke, trans., *Catherine of Siena: The Dialogue*, The Classics of Western Spirituality (New York: Paulist Press, 1980), 366.

TRINITY

HILDEGARD OF BINGEN

He Who Is, and from Whom nothing is hidden, says, O shepherd, do not allow the sweet flow of the odor of balsam dry up in you, that vitality which must be given to the foolish who do not have the breasts of maternal compassion to suck, and who, therefore, lack sustenance. Therefore, offer the lamp of the King to your people, so that they might not be scattered in bitterness, and you yourself rise up, living, in its light.

Father, I, a poor little woman, am able to expound upon the question you asked me, because I have looked to the True Light, and I am sending along to you the answer I saw and heard in a true vision—not my words, I remind you, but those of the True Light, which has no imperfection.

Eternity is the essential quality of the Father. That is to say, nothing can be added or subtracted from it, for eternity is like a wheel, which has neither beginning nor end. Thus, in the Father, before the beginning of the world, eternity is. Eternity always is and always has been. What is eternity? It is God. For eternity is not eternity except in Perfect Life. Therefore, God lives in eternity. Life proceeds not from mortality, but life is in life. Thus a tree grows only from its life-giving sap, and not even a stone is without its moisture, and every living thing has its own life force. For eternity is itself alive, and is not without the ability to produce life.

How is this so? It was the function of the Word of the Father to bring forth every created thing. And so the Father is not idle in his great might. Hence, God is called the Father, because all things are born from Him. And so, once again, eternity is an essential quality of the Father, because He was Father before the beginning, and was eternal before the inception of His magnificent works, all of which He foresaw eternally. But the state of the Father is not the state of man, which is sometimes uncertain, sometimes past, sometimes future, sometimes new, sometimes old, but that which is in the Father is always stable.

The Father is brightness, and that brightness has radiance, and that radiance has fire: and they are all one. Whoever does not believe this does not see God, because he is seeking to make a division in an indivisible God. Indeed, the works which God established no longer have their undivided essence, since man has brought about divisions.

Brightness is Paternity, from which all things have their being and by which they are all embraced, for they derive from its power. That same power made man, and breathed the breath of life into him. But also in that same power man has his own potency. How? Flesh produces flesh, and good propagates that which is good: the good is spread abroad by spiritual conversation and is increased by good example in another person. These powers are in man both carnally and spiritually, because one thing proceeds from another. Man highly prizes his useful works, because he conceives them in his mind and brings them into effect by his actions. So, too, it is God's will that His power be manifested in all his creatures, because they are His work.

Radiance gives eyes, and that Radiance which is the Son gave eyes when he said, "Let there be." At that moment all things appeared physically in the Living Eye. And fire, which is God, permeates these two terms, because it is impossible to have brightness without radiance. And if they did not have fire, there would be neither brightness nor radiance. Flame and light lie hidden in fire; otherwise it would not be fire.

Equality is the essential characteristic of the Son. How? All creatures were in the Father before the beginning of time, all in the order He Himself had ordained. Afterward, the Son gave them their physical form. How? All creatures were in the Father before the beginning of time, all in the order He Himself had ordained. Afterward, the Son gave them their physical form. How? It is like a person who conceives an idea of a great work, and then makes it explicit by his word so that it comes forth in praiseworthy form.

The Father ordains, the Son puts into effect. For the Father has ordained all things in Himself, and the Son has brought them to completion. And the light which was in the beginning is from that eternal light before the beginning of the world, and this light, whose radiance is from the Father, is the Son, through Whom all things were made. And the Son clothed Himself in the garment of mankind, whom he had formed from the mud, the garment which, before, had no bodily form. Thus God saw all his works before Him as light, and when He said "Let there be," He gave each kind its own proper garment. . . .

The connection between eternity and equality is the Holy Spirit. The Holy Spirit is a fire, but it is not an extinguishable fire that sometimes blazes up and sometimes is put out. It permeates eternity and equality, and binds the two into one, just as a person binds together a bundle of sticks (which, if not bound, flies all asunder). And it is like a blacksmith who unites the two materials of bronze and makes them one through fire. It is a sword brandished in every direction. The Holy Spirit reveals eternity and enkindles equality, joining them into one. The Holy Spirit is fire and life in eternity and equality, because God is living. The sun is radiant with a blazing light, and the fire burns in it. It illuminates the whole world, and it appears as a single entity. But any thing devoid of life-force is dead, just as a limb cut off from a tree becomes withered, because it no longer has the stuff of life in it.

The Holy Spirit is the uniting factor and the life-giving force, for without the Holy Spirit eternity would not be eternity, nor would equality be equality. The Holy Spirit is in both, and the three are one in divinity, that is, God is one.

Joseph L. Baird and Radd K. Ehrman, trans., *The Letters of Hildegard of Bingen* (New York: Oxford University Press, 1994), 95–96, 97.

TRINITY

HILDEGARD OF BINGEN

Next I saw a very bright light, and inside it there was a person who was the color of a sapphire. The bright light signifies God who is without any blemish of illusion, defect, and falsehood. The person signifies the Word who is without any blemish of hard-heartedness, ill will, and unfairness. The Word was begotten before time according to the divinity of God, but the Word was made flesh afterwards in time according to the humanity of the world. This person was completely surrounded by a very pleasant fire of reddish color. This fire signifies the Holy Spirit who is without any blemish of dryness, death, and darkness. The Only-Begotten of God was conceived in flesh from the Holy Spirit and was born within time from the Virgin—the light of true brightness poured out into the world. The very bright light completely surrounded this fire of reddish color, and at the same time this fire completely surrounded the light. Both the fire and the light surrounded the person, existing as one light with one force of potentiality. This signifies that God, the Word, and the Holy Spirit are inseparable in the majesty of their divinity. God is the most just justice, but is not without the Word and the Holy Spirit. The Word is the fullness of fruitfulness, but is not without God and the Holy Spirit. The Holy Spirit is the attendant of faithful hearts, but is not without God and the Word. For God is not without the Word, nor the Word without God, and neither God nor the Word are without the Holy Spirit.

And the Holy Spirit is not without God and the Word. All of these three persons exist as one in the whole divinity of majesty. The unity of the divinity flourishes in God—neither God nor the Word without the Holy Spirit, nor the Holy Spirit without them. These three persons exist as one in the whole divinity of majesty, and the unity of divinity flourishes in these three inseparable persons because divinity is not able to be split since that exists without any change. God is shown through the Word, the Word through the birth of creatures, and the Holy Spirit through the Word being made flesh. What does this mean? God is the one who begot the Word before time, the Word is the one through whom all things from God have been done in creatures, and the Holy Spirit is the one who appeared in the form of a dove at the baptism of the Word who existed in time for a certain amount of time.

Bruce Hozeski, trans., *Hildegard von Bingen's Mystical Visions: Translated from Scivias,* introduced by Matthew Fox (Santa Fe: Bear & Company, 1995), 87–88.

TRINITY

MECHTHILD OF MAGDEBURG

Let him [Christ] open to me the joyful flow
that runs within the Holy Trinity,
the soul's only source of life. . . .
For the blissful Sun of the living Godhead
shines through the pure water of happy Humanity,
and the sweet joy of the Holy Spirit
proceeds from the one and from the other.

José De Vinck, *Revelations of Women Mystics: From Middle Ages to Modern Times* (New York: Alba House, 1985), 9.

VIRTUE

CATHERINE OF SIENA

[God says:] You see, then, that the demons are my ministers to torment the damned in hell and to exercise and test your virtue in this life. Not that it is the devil's intention to make you prove your virtue (for he has no charity). He would rather deprive you of virtue! But he cannot, unless you will it so.

How great is the stupidity of those who make themselves weak in spite of my strengthening, and put themselves into the devil's hands! I want you to know, then, that at the moment of death, because they have put themselves during life under the devil's rule (not by force, because they cannot be forced, as I told you; but they put themselves voluntarily into his hands), and because they come to the point of death under this perverse rule, they can expect no other judgment but that of their own conscience. They come without hope to eternal damnation. In hate they grasp at hell in the moment of their death, and even before they possess it, they take hell as their prize along with their lords the demons.

The just, on the other hand, have lived in charity and die in love. If they have lived perfectly in virtue, enlightened by faith, seeing with faith and trusting completely in the blood of the Lamb, when they come to the point of death they see the good I have prepared for them. They embrace it with the arms of love, reaching out with the grasp of love to me, the supreme and eternal Good, at the very edge of death. And so they taste eternal life even before they have left their mortal bodies.

Suzanne Noffke, trans., *Catherine of Siena: The Dialogue,* The Classics of Western Spirituality (New York: Paulist Press, 1980), 88–89.

Virtue

Hadewijch of Antwerp (Brabant)

It was a Sunday, in the Octave of Pentecost, when our Lord was brought secretly to my bedside, because I felt such an attraction of my spirit inwardly that I could not control myself outwardly in a degree sufficient to go among persons; it would have been impossible for me to go among them. And that desire which I had inwardly was to be one with God in fruition. For this I was still too childish and too little grown-up; and I had not as yet sufficiently suffered for it or lived the number of years requisite for such exceptional worthiness. That is what was shown me then and still seems the same to me. When I had received our Lord, he then received me to him, so that he withdrew my senses from every remembrance of alien things to enable me to have joy in him in inward togetherness with him. Then I was led as if into a meadow, an expanse that was called the space of perfect virtue. In it stood trees, and I was guided close to them. And I was shown their names and the significance of their names.

The first tree had a rotten root, which was very brittle, but a very solid trunk. And above this bloomed a charming, very beautiful flower; but it was so frail that if a storm had ever blown up, this flower would have fallen and faded. He who guided me was an Angel belonging to the choir of Thrones (cf. Col. 1:16), the very ones who are charged with discernment. And this same day, having grown up, I had come close to him, so that I had received him; and from then on he was to be my guardian and the companion of all my ways. And this Angel said: "Human nature, understand and know what this tree is!" And I understood, just as he revealed it to me, that the tree was the knowledge of ourselves. The rotten root was our brittle nature; the solid trunk, the eternal soul; and the beautiful flower, the beautiful human shape, which becomes corrupt so quickly, in an instant (cf. James 1:11).

Mother Columba Hart, trans., *Hadewijch: The Complete Works,* The Classics of Western Spirituality (New York: Paulist Press, 1980), 263.

Virtue

Teresa of Avila

It was a wonderful thing for me to have received the grace which God had granted me through prayer, for this made me realize what it was to love Him. After a short time I found these virtues were renewed within me, although not in great strength, for they were not sufficient to uphold me in righteousness. I never spoke ill of anyone in the slightest degree, for my usual practice was to avoid all evil-speaking. I used to remind myself that I must not wish or say anything about anyone which I should not like to be said of me. I was extremely particular about observing this rule on all possible occasions, although I was not so perfect as not to fail now and then when faced with difficult situations. Still, that was my usual habit; and those who were with me and had to do with me were so much struck by it that they made it a habit too. It came to be realized that in my presence people could turn their backs to me and yet be quite safe; and so, too, they were with my friends and kinsfolk and those who learned from me.

E. Allison Peers, trans. and ed., *The Life of Teresa of Jesus: The Autobiography of Teresa of Avila* (New York: Image Books/Doubleday, 1991), 91.

Visions

Angela of Foligno

On the Sunday before the feast of the Indulgence, a Mass was being celebrated at the altar of the most reverend Virgin Mary in the upper church of the basilica of blessed Francis. At about the time of the elevation of the body of the Lord, while the organ was playing the angelic hymn "Holy, holy, holy," Angela's soul was absorbed and transported into the uncreated light by the majestic power of the sovereign and uncreated God. The result of this ecstasy was such fruition and illumination as is totally indescribable. What is said here of this experience captures absolutely nothing of it, for no human words are eloquent enough to express the way the uncreated and omnipotent God powerfully draws the soul to himself. After her absorption into the fathomless depths of God and while she was still under the impact of this continuing vision, the image of the blessed crucified God and man appeared to her, looking as if he just then been taken down from the cross. His blood flowed fresh and crimson as if the wounds had just recently been opened. Then she saw how the joints and tendons of his blessed body were torn and distended by the cruel stretching and pulling of his virginal limbs at the hands of those who had set upon him to kill him on the gibbet of the cross. The bones and sinews of his most holy body seemed completely torn out of their natural position; and yet his skin was not broken.

At this heartrending sight she was transfixed to the marrow with such compassion that in truth it seemed to her that she was totally transformed in spirit and body into the pain of the cross. At the sight of the dislocated limbs and the painful distension of the sinews, she felt herself pierced through even more than she had been at the sight of the open wounds. For the former granted her a deeper insight into the secret of his passion and the harsh cruelty of his executioners. The sight of the crucified body of the good and beloved Jesus stirred her to such compassion that when she saw it, all her own joints seemed to cry out with fresh laments, and her whole body and soul felt pierced anew from the painful impact of this divine vision. She was in a daze, because on the one hand, the uncreated God was refreshing and restoring her soul with the ineffable radiance of his most sweet divinity's fathomless splendor, but on the other hand, the same blessed crucified God and man, Jesus, pierced her whole being with his compassionate crucifixion and his cruel death pains which he showed her. Thus the blessed and glorious Jesus, by an invisible act, had fittingly bestowed upon her soul, in a perfect manner, the double state of his own life. He did this by granting her a certain intuition which, through the transformative power of her compassion over his death, allowed her full contemplation of his life and crucifixion. For more than any one I have ever seen, she strove to outwardly conform herself totally to the life of Christ. But let us refrain from trying to praise her—for no words can be found to match her virtues.

Paul Lachance, trans., *Angela of Foligno: Complete Works,* The Classics of Western Spirituality (Mahwah, N.J.: Paulist Press, 1993), 245-46.

VISIONS

HILDEGARD OF BINGEN

When I was forty-two years and seven months old, a burning light of tremendous brightness coming from heaven poured into my entire mind. Like a flame that does not burn but enkindles, it inflamed my entire heart and my entire breast, just like the sun that warms an object with its rays.... All of a sudden, I was able to taste of the understanding of the narration of books. I saw the psalter clearly and the evangelist and other catholic books of the Old and New Testaments.

Matthew Fox, *Illuminations of Hildegard of Bingen* (Santa Fe: Bear & Company, 1985), 9.

VISIONS

JULIAN OF NORWICH

But I lay still awake, and then our Lord opened my spiritual eyes, and showed me my soul in the midst of my heart. I saw my soul as wide as if it were a kingdom, and from the state which I saw in it, it seemed to me as if it were a fine city. In the midst of this city sits our Lord Jesus, true God and true man, a handsome person and tall, honourable, the greatest lord. And I saw him splendidly clad in honours. He sits erect there in the soul, in peace and rest, and he rules and he guards heaven and earth and everything that is. The humanity and the divinity sit at rest, and the divinity rules and guards, without instrument or effort. And my soul is blessedly occupied by the divinity, sovereign power, sovereign wisdom, sovereign goodness.

The place which Jesus takes in our soul he will nevermore vacate, for in us is his home of homes, and it is the greatest delight for him to dwell there. This was a delectable and a restful sight, for it is so in truth forevermore; and to contemplate this while we are here is most pleasing to God, and very great profit to us. And the soul who thus contemplates is made like to him who is contemplated, and united to him in rest and peace. And it was a singular joy and bliss to me that I saw him sit, for the contemplation of this sitting revealed to me the certainty that he will dwell in us forever; and I knew truly that it was he who had revealed everything to me before. And when I had contemplated this with great attention, our Lord very humbly revealed words to me, without voice and without opening of lips, as he had done before, and said very seriously: Know it well, it was no hallucination which you saw today, but accept and believe it and hold firmly to it, and you will not be overcome.

These last words were said to me to teach me perfect certainty that it is our Lord Jesus who revealed everything to me; for just as in the first words which our Lord revealed to me, alluding to his blessed Passion: With this the fiend is overcome, just so he said with perfect certainty in these last words: You will not be overcome. And this teaching and this true strengthening apply generally to all my fellow Christians, as I have said before, and so is the will of God.

And these words: You will not be overcome, were said very insistently and strongly, for certainty and strength against every tribulation which may come. He did not say: You will not be assailed, you will not be belaboured, you will not be disquieted, but he said: You will not be overcome. God wants us to pay attention to his words, and always to be strong in our certainty, in well-being and in woe, for he loves us and delights in us, and so he wishes us to love him and delight in him and trust greatly in him, and all will be well.

And soon afterwards all was hidden, and I saw no more.

Edmund Colledge and James Walsh, trans., *Julian of Norwich: Showings*, The Classics of Western Spirituality (New York: Paulist Press, 1978), 163–65.

VISIONS

MARGARET EBNER

Around that time I had a vision while sleeping. I was standing beneath a window and the gentlest breeze arose with uncommonly strong power. From this same power three utterly clear streams of water began to flow. The earth was covered by mounds, representing the sins of men. And the streams were flowing against these mounds. The water was so powerful that it was amazing that these mounds were not broken up by the water. Indeed many remained undisturbed. When all those that lay in the valley were washed away completely, a beautiful green pasture appeared. I was given to understand: Those who lay in the valley were the humble. Then one of our holy women, who is now with God, stood there and said to me, "See now that your Lord can show Himself as Lord indeed."

Leonard Hindsley, trans. and ed., *Margaret Ebner: Major Works*, The Classics of Western Spirituality (Mahwah, N.J.: Paulist Press, 1993), 94.

Visions

Margaret Ebner

On Shrove Tuesday I was in choir late after Vespers and was praying in front of the altar. Before me eyes I saw three lights, round like disks. Then I received the great grace with immeasurable joy from the presence of God. And the Speaking came upon me again. The whole of Lent I spent in great, sweet grace and inner desire to serve God in choir and in all places. I often had the special desire to press and kiss and drink from the five wounds of my Beloved Jesus Christ whenever I made a profound inclination. In the sweet Name of Jesus Christ I was also compelled sometimes to say "Jesus Christus" after each verse of the psalms. I yearned greatly to speak about the grace of our Lord, but I had no one to tell, because the Friend of our Lord, who had been given to me by His goodness for powerful consolation, remained in Avignon.

Leonard Hindsley, trans. and ed., *Margaret Ebner: Major Works,* The Classics of Western Spirituality (Mahwah, N.J.: Paulist Press, 1993), 107-8.

Visions

Margaret Ebner

The light about which I have written has appeared to me often since then. Sometimes a light was given to me that shoots out from my eyes like flames; at other times I am given small lights. But what all these lights mean, only the true Light, Jesus Christ, knows well. From them I received great sweetness and divine delight.

Leonard Hindsley, trans. and ed., *Margaret Ebner: Major Works,* The Classics of Western Spirituality (Mahwah, N.J.: Paulist Press, 1993), 110.

VISIONS

MARGARET EBNER

I was asleep on All Souls' Day and it seemed to me as if I had come into a strange place. There I found many sorts of deceased people whom I knew. And with great desire they asked me to pray to God for them. After that I came to a beautiful green place where there were tall trees from which beautiful apples were falling. I saw people whom I knew well and about whom I firmly believe and trust that they enjoy eternal life. Then two others, who were sisters of our monastery, came over to me. They gave me two of the apples. One of them was sour, the other sweet. They asked me to eat them. I took the apples and bit into them. Then I felt such great grace from the apples that I said, "No one on earth could eat both." They said, "If you do not like them, give them back to us." Then I awoke still chewing, and the grace was so sweet and so strong that I could not speak a word and could not take in breath and was really without any of my bodily senses.

Leonard Hindsley, trans. and ed., *Margaret Ebner: Major Works*, The Classics of Western Spirituality (Mahwah, N.J.: Paulist Press, 1993), 171.

VOCATION

CATHERINE OF GENOA

So that you will have something to do, God said to her,

> you will work for a living.
> You [Catherine] will be asked to do works of
>   charity
> among the poor sick,
> and when asked you will clean filthy things.
> Should you be conversing with God at the time

you will leave all and not ask who sends for you
   or needs you.
Do not do your will but that of others.
You will have the time you need,
for I intend to crush all disordered pleasures and
   discipline you—
and I want to see results.
If I find that you consider some things repugnant
I will have you so concentrate on them
that they will no longer be such.
I will also take away
all those things that gave you some comfort
and make you die to them.
The better to test you,
I will have you endure a corresponding version
   in spiritual things
of those that give and take away pleasure.
You will have no friendships, no special family
   ties.
You will love everyone without love,
rich and poor, friends and relatives.
You are not to make friends,
not even spiritual or religious friendships,
or go to see anyone out of friendship.
It is enough that you go when you are called,
as I told you before.
This is the way you are to consort with your
   fellow creatures on earth.

Serge Hughes, trans., *Catherine of Genoa: Purgation and Purgatory, The Spiritual Dialogue,* The Classics of Western Spirituality (New York: Paulist Press, 1979), 128-29.

VOCATION

CATHERINE OF GENOA

Empty of any support or refreshment within, completely alienated, Human Frailty said to the Spirit:

> If you want me to do this work, give me the
>   strength to do it.
> I will not shrink from anything,
> but to do this work well, love is needed.

Serge Hughes, trans., *Catherine of Genoa: Purgation and Purgatory, The Spiritual Dialogue,* The Classics of Western Spirituality (New York: Paulist Press, 1979), 132.

VOCATION

CATHERINE OF SIENA

[God says:] You are the workers I have hired for the vineyard of holy Church. When I gave you the light of holy baptism I sent you by my grace to work in the universal body of Christianity. You received your baptism within the mystic body of holy Church by the hands of my ministers, and these ministers I have sent to work with you. You are to work in the universal body. They, however, have been placed within the mystic body to shepherd your souls by administering the blood to you through the sacraments you receive from them, and by rooting out from you the thorns of deadly sin and planting grace within you. They are my workers in the vineyard of your souls, ambassadors for the vineyard of holy Church.

Each of your has your own vineyard, your soul, in which your free will is the appointed worker during this life. Once the time of your life has passed, your will can work neither for good nor for evil; but while you live it can till the vineyard of your soul where I have placed it. This tiller of your soul has been given such power that neither the devil nor any other creature can steal it without the will's consent, for in holy baptism the will was armed with a knife that is love of virtue and hatred of sin. This love and hatred are to be found in the blood. For my only-begotten Son gave his blood for you in death out of love for you and hatred of sin, and through that blood you receive life in holy baptism.

Suzanne Noffke, trans., *Catherine of Siena: The Dialogue,* The Classics of Western Spirituality (New York: Paulist Press, 1980), 60.

VOCATION

CATHERINE OF SIENA

[God says:] So you have this knife for your free will to use, while you have time, to uproot the thorns of deadly sin and to plant the virtues. This is the only way you can receive the fruit of the blood from these workers I have placed in holy Church. For they are there, as I have told you, to uproot deadly sin from the vineyard of your soul and to give you grace by administering the blood to you through the sacraments established in holy Church.

So if you would receive the fruit of this blood, you must first rouse yourself to heartfelt contrition, contempt for sin, and love for virtue. Otherwise you will not have done your part to be fit to be joined as branches to the vine that is my only-begotten Son, who said, "I am the true vine and you are the branches. And my Father is the gardener."

Indeed I am the gardener, for all that exists comes from me. With power and strength beyond imagining I govern the whole world: Not a thing is made or kept in order without me. I am the gardener, then, who planted the vine of my only-begotten Son in the earth of your humanity so that you, the branches, could be joined to the vine and bear fruit.

Suzanne Noffke, trans., *Catherine of Siena: The Dialogue,* The Classics of Western Spirituality (New York: Paulist Press, 1980), 60–61.

VOCATION

CATHERINE OF SIENA

[God says:] Therefore, if you do not produce the fruit of good and holy deeds you will be cut off from this vine and you will dry up. For those who are cut off from this vine lose the life of grace and are thrown into the eternal fire, just as a branch that fails to bear fruit is cut off the vine and thrown into the fire, since it is good for nothing else. So those who are cut off because of their offenses, if they die still guilty of deadly sin, will be thrown into the fire that lasts forever, for they are good for nothing else.

Such people have not tilled their vineyards. They have, in fact, destroyed them—yes, and other people's as well. Not only did they fail to set out any good plants of virtue, but they even dug out the seed of grace that they had received with the light of holy baptism, when they had drunk of the blood of my Son—that wine poured out for you by this true vine. They dug out this seed and fed it to beasts, that is, to their countless sins. And they trampled it underfoot with their disordered will, and so offended me and brought harm to their neighbors as well as to themselves.

But that is not how my servants act, and you should be like them, joined and engrafted to this vine. Then you will produce much fruit, because you will share the vital sap of the vine. And being in the Word, my Son, you will be in me, for I am one with him and he with me. If you are in him you will follow his teaching, and if you follow his teaching you will share in the very being of this Word—that is, you will share in the eternal Godhead made one with humanity, whence you will draw that divine love which inebriates the soul. All this I mean when I say that you will share in the very substance of the vine.

Do you know what course I follow, once my servants have completely given themselves to the teaching of the gentle loving Word? I prune them, so that they will bear much fruit—cultivated fruit, not wild. Just as the gardener prunes the branch that is joined to the vine so that it will yield more and better wine, but cuts off and throws into the fire the branch that is barren, so do I the true gardener act. When my servants remain united to me I prune them with great suffering so that they will bear more and better fruit, and virtue will be proved in them. But those who bear no fruit are cut off and thrown into the fire.

These are the true workers. They till their souls well, uprooting every selfish love, cultivating the soil of their love in me. They feed and tend the growth of the seed of grace that they received in holy baptism. And as they till their own vineyards, so they till their neighbors' as well, for they cannot do the one without the other. You already know that every evil as well as every good is done by means of your neighbors.

Suzanne Noffke, trans., *Catherine of Siena: The Dialogue,* The Classics of Western Spirituality (New York: Paulist Press, 1980), 61–62.

VOCATION

CATHERINE OF SIENA

[God says:] You, then, are my workers. You have come from me, the supreme eternal gardener, and I have engrafted you onto the vine by making myself one with you.

Keep in mind that each of you has your own vineyard. But every one is joined to your neighbors' vineyards without any dividing lines. They are so joined together, in fact, that you cannot do good or evil for yourself without doing the same for your neighbors.

All of you together make up one common vineyard, the whole Christian assembly, and you are all united in the vineyard of the mystic body of holy Church from which you draw your life. In this vineyard is planted the vine, which is my only-begotten Son, into whom you must be engrafted. Unless you are engrafted into him you are rebels against holy Church, like members that are cut off from the body and rot.

It is true that while you have time you can get yourselves out of the stench of sin through true repentance and recourse to my ministers. They are the workers who have the keys to the wine cellar, that is, the blood poured forth from this vine. (And this blood is so perfect in itself that you cannot be deprived of its benefits through any fault in the minister.)

It is charity that binds you to true humility—the humility that is found in knowing yourself and me. See, then, that it is as workers that I have sent you all. And now I am calling you again, because the world is failing fast. The thorns have so multiplied and have choked the seed so badly that it will produce no fruit of grace at all.

I want you, therefore, to be true workers. With deep concern help to till the souls in the mystic body of holy Church. I am calling you to this because I want to be merciful to the world as you have so earnestly begged me.

Suzanne Noffke, trans., *Catherine of Siena: The Dialogue,* The Classics of Western Spirituality (New York: Paulist Press, 1980), 62-63.

Vocation

Hildegard of Bingen

When you compassionately touch and cleanse the wounds of others, then I [love] am reclining on your bed. And when you meet simple, honest people with good will and in a godly way, then I am united to you in loving friendship. . . . I, wisdom, bind together heavenly and earthly things as a unity for the good of the people. And so you should handle and cleanse the wounds of those who are sick; and you should maintain the innocent and righteous. And with God's help let your heart rejoice with the one as much as the other.

Matthew Fox, *Illuminations of Hildegard of Bingen* (Santa Fe: Bear & Company, 1985), 24.

VOCATION

HILDEGARD OF BINGEN

What can you accomplish along with me? Clearly, the most brilliant of works. Works that are more brilliant than the splendor of the sun and are sweeter in inner taste than milk and honey.... For when you desire me with the innermost understanding of your soul, as you have been taught in baptism through faith, do I not make whole what you desire?

Matthew Fox, *Illuminations of Hildegard of Bingen* (Santa Fe: Bear & Company, 1985), 100.

VOCATION

JULIAN OF NORWICH

Before this time I had often great longing, and desired of God's gift to be delivered from this world and this life, for I wanted to be with my God in the bliss in which I surely hope to be without end. For often I beheld the woe that there is here, and the good and the blessed life that is there; and if there had been no other pain on earth except the absence of our Lord God, it seemed to me sometimes that that would be more than I could bear. And this made me mourn and diligently long.

Then God said to me, for my patience and endurance: Suddenly you will be taken out of all your pain, all your unrest and all your woe. And you will come up above, and you will have me for your reward, and you will be filled full of joy and bliss, and you will never have any kind of pain, any kind of sickness, any kind of displeasure, any kind of disappointment, but always endless joy and bliss. Why then should it grieve you to endure for awhile, since it is my will and to my glory?

As God reasoned with me—"Suddenly you will be taken"—I saw how he rewards men for their patience in awaiting the time of his will, and how men have patience to endure throughout the span of their lives, because they do not know when the time for them to die will come. This is very profitable, because if they knew when that would be, they would set a limit to their patience. Then, too, it is God's will that so long as the soul is in the body it should seem to a man that he is always on the point of being taken. For all this life and all the longing we have here is only an instant of time, and when we are suddenly taken into bliss out of pain, it will be nothing.

Therefore our Lord said: Why then should it grieve you to endure for a while, since that is my will and to my glory? It is God's will that we accept his commands and his consolations as generously and as fully as we are able; and he also wants us to accept our tarrying and our suffering as lightly as we are able, and to count them as nothing. For the more lightly we accept them, the less importance we ascribe to them because of our love, the less pain shall we experience from them and the more thanks shall we have for them.

In this blessed revelation I was truly taught that any man or woman who voluntarily chooses God in his lifetime may be sure that he too is chosen. Pay true heed to this, for it is indeed God's will for us to be as certain in our trust to have the bliss of heaven whilst we are here as we shall be certain of it when we are there.

And always, the more delight and joy that we accept from this certainty, with reverence and humility, the more pleasing it is to God. For I am certain that if there had been no one but I to be saved, God would have done everything which he has done for me. And so ought every soul to think, acknowledging who it is who loves him, forgetting if he can the rest of creation, and thinking that God has done everything he has done for him. And it seems to me that this ought to move a soul to love him and delight in him, and to fear nothing but him; for it is his will that we know that all the power of our enemy is shut in the hand of our friend. And therefore a soul that knows this to be sure will fear nothing but him whom he loves, and count all other fears among the sufferings and bodily sicknesses and illusions which he must endure.

Edmund Colledge and James Walsh, trans., *Julian of Norwich: Showings,* The Classics of Western Spirituality (New York: Paulist Press, 1978), 160–61.

VOCATION

TERESA OF AVILA

During this time, when I was considering these resolutions, I had persuaded one of my brothers, by talking to him about the vanity of the world, to become a friar, and we agreed to set out together, very early one morning, for the convent where that friend of mine lived of whom I was so fond. In making my final decision, I had already resolved that I would go to any convent in which I thought I could serve God better or which my father might wish me to enter, for by now I was concerned chiefly with the good of my soul and cared nothing for my comfort. I remember—and I really believe this is true—that when I left my father's house my distress was so great that I do not think it will be greater when I die. It seemed to me as if every bone in my body were being wrenched asunder; for, as I had no love of God to subdue my love for my father and kinsfolk, everything was such a strain to me that, if the Lord had not helped me, no reflections of my own would have sufficed to keep me true to my purpose. But the Lord gave me courage to fight against myself and so I carried out my intention.

E. Allison Peers, trans. and ed., *The Life of Teresa of Jesus: The Autobiography of Teresa of Avila* (New York: Image Books/Doubleday, 1991), 76–77.

VOCATION

TERESA OF AVILA

When I took the habit, the Lord at once showed me how great are His favours to those who use force with themselves in His service. No one realized that I had gone through all this; they all thought I had acted out of sheer desire. At the time my entrance into this new life gave me a joy so great that it has never failed me even to this day, and God converted the aridity of my soul into the deepest tenderness. Everything connected with the religious life caused me delight; and it is a fact that sometimes, when I was spending time in sweeping floors which I had previously spent on my own indulgence and adornment, and realized that I was now free from all those things, there came to me a new joy, which amazed me, for I could not understand whence it arose. Whenever I recall this, there is nothing, however hard, which I would hesitate to undertake if it were proposed to me. For I know now, by experience of many kinds, that if I strengthen my purpose by resolving to do a thing for God's sake alone, it is His will that, from the very beginning, my soul shall be afraid, so that my merit may be the greater; and if I achieve my resolve, the greater my fear has been, the greater will be my reward, and the greater, too, will be my retrospective pleasure. Even in this life His Majesty rewards such an act in ways that can be understood only by one who has enjoyed them. This I know by experience, as I have said, in many very serious matters; and so, if I were a person who had to advise others, I would never recommend anyone, when a good inspiration comes to him again and again, to hesitate to put it into practice because of fear; for, if one lives a life of detachment for God's sake alone, there is no reason to be afraid that things will turn out amiss, since He is all-powerful. May He be blessed for ever. Amen.

E. Allison Peers, trans. and ed., *The Life of Teresa of Jesus: The Autobiography of Teresa of Avila* (New York: Image Books/Doubleday, 1991), 77–78.

VOICE

HILDEGARD OF BINGEN

I am forced to write these words regarding which I would have gladly kept silent because I fear greatly the power of vain-glory. But I have learned to fear more the judgment of God should I, God's small creature, keep silent.

Matthew Fox, *Illuminations of Hildegard of Bingen* (Santa Fe: Bear & Company, 1985), 13.

VOICE

HILDEGARD OF BINGEN

And a heavenly voice spoke to me:

> You will not be able to see anything more fully concerning this mystery unless it is granted to you on account of the miracle of your believing.

Next I saw a very peaceful person going out from the brightness of the previously mentioned dawn. This person poured light into the darkness. With the redness of blood and in the whiteness of paleness, this person drove this darkness upward with great strength. This person—having been hurled through the darkness and having touched it—became visible, was bright, was lifted up, and went forth. This very peaceful person spoke aloud with human language. This person brought forth endless glory on high and sent forth a wondrous fruitfulness and odor. Again the voice from the previously mentioned living fire spoke to me:

> O you who are miserable on earth and have the name of a woman, you have not been taught any of the doctrines of the fleshly masters. But you have collected your knowl-

edge from the intelligence of the philosophers. You have been touched by my light inwardly. My fire burns like the sun. Cry aloud and explain and write these mysteries of mine which you see and hear in this mystical vision. Do not be timid. Speak these things which you understand in the spirit, so that I may speak these things through you. Have the modesty of those who ought to show my righteousness to my people. Some refuse to speak what they know because of their wanton ways. They do not wish to drag themselves away from their evil desires which control them and make them flee from the face of the Lord. They blush and do not want to speak the truth. But you, o tiny soul, have been taught inwardly by my mystical inspiration. Although you have been trampled under foot in your human form on account of the sin of Eve, speak nevertheless about the fiery work which has been shown to you most clearly.

For the living God who had created all things through a Word, through the same Word having been made incarnate, led the wretched human creature, who had plunged into darkness, back to faithful salvation.

Bruce Hozeski, trans., *Hildegard von Bingen's Mystical Visions: Translated from Scivias,* introduced by Matthew Fox (Santa Fe: Bear & Company, 1995), 78–79.

WISDOM

HADEWIJCH OF ANTWERP (BRABANT)

Be prompt and zealous in every virtue,
But do not apply yourself to any single one.
Do not neglect any work,
But do not devote yourself to any particular one.
Be kind and compassionate towards every need,
But do not give your special care to any.

Emilie Zum Brunn and Georgette Epiney-Burgard, *Women Mystics in Medieval Europe* (New York: Paragon House, 1989), 122.

WISDOM

HADEWIJCH OF ANTWERP (BRABANT)

This tree was wisdom. The first lowest branch, which had the red hearts on its leaves, signified the fear of not being perfect and of forsaking perfect virtues. The second branch was the fear that persons do not show God many marks of homage, and that such a number go astray from the Truth, which is himself. The third branch was the fear that each person must die by the same death whereby our Beloved died, with wisdom to be perfect in each and every virtue in order to die of that death every hour, and to carry that cross, and to die on it each day, and to die with all those who go astray and die.

Mother Columba Hart, trans., *Hadewijch: The Complete Works,* The Classics of Western Spirituality (New York: Paulist Press, 1980), 265.

WISDOM

HILDEGARD OF BINGEN

Know the wise ways as distinct from the foolish ways. [People who follow the ways of wisdom] will themselves become a fountain gushing from the waters of life.... For these waters—that is, the believers—are a spring that can never be exhausted or run dry. No one will ever have too much of them ... the waters through which we have been reborn to life have been sprinkled by the Holy Spirit.

Matthew Fox, *Illuminations of Hildegard of Bingen* (Santa Fe: Bear & Company, 1985), 9-10.

142

WISDOM

MARGARET EBNER

The next day I was very sick and began to wonder about
what was happening to me. I perceived well what it was. It
came from my heart and I feared for my senses now and
then whenever it was so intense. But I was answered by
the presence of God with sweet delight, "I am no robber of
the senses, I am the enlightener of the senses." I received a
great grace from the inner goodness of God: the light of
truth of divine understanding. Also my mind became more
rational than before, so that I had the grace to be able to
phrase all my speech better and also to understand better
all speech according to the truth. Since then I am often
talked about. Often I responded to others according to the
truth rather than according to their words. About this gift
and many other gifts which were given to me I cannot write
now; later I shall write about them as they increase in me.
All this happened on the Tuesday when the grasp of love
took my heart, as I should have mentioned in the beginning. The grace of our Lord was so very powerful in me
and was so unknown to my weak senses that I fell down
before our Lord and yielded myself to His divine grace.

Leonard Hindsley, trans. and ed., *Margaret Ebner: Major Works,* The Classics of
Western Spirituality (Mahwah, N.J.: Paulist Press, 1993), 100.

WORSHIP

HILDEGARD OF BINGEN

Ceaselessly we must praise the Heavenly Creator with the voice of both mouth and heart, for, by His grace, He receives in the celestial dwellings not only those who stand erect, but also those who fall and those who are bent. And so behold, O man, that very luminous air which betells the radiant joy of the heavenly citizens, an air which, in a marvelous manner, transmits to your ears (in accordance with the symbols explained above) the different kinds of music by which those of the faithful who have courageously persevered in the way of truth sing the joys of Heaven, together with those who, with lamentations of repentance, have been led back to the praise of these celestial joys.

Emilie Zum Brunn and Georgette Epiney-Burgard, *Women Mystics in Medieval Europe* (New York: Paragon House, 1989), 35.

WORSHIP

HILDEGARD OF BINGEN

Be not lax in celebrating. Be not lazy in the festive service of God. Be ablaze with enthusiasm. Let us be an alive, burning offering before the altar of God!

Matthew Fox, *Illuminations of Hildegard of Bingen* (Santa Fe: Bear & Company, 1985), 115.

Biographical Sketches

ANGELA OF FOLIGNO

Angela of Foligno, the great Italian mystic, was born in 1248 in Foligno, a town very near Assisi in Italy. Angela, known also as "Lella," was born of well-to-do parents. Her father, possibly a nobleman, died when she was a child. At age 20 she married and subsequently had several sons.

Few details are known about her life prior to 1285, although it is clear from her writings that she was intelligent, cultured, impetuous, and passionate. She described herself as living a privileged, superficial, and pleasure-seeking life before she entered the way of penance in 1285. In the *Memorial,* which narrates her story, she describes this decisive point in her life when she was 37. At that time she was overcome with bitter weeping and "the fear of being damned to hell" for her sinful life. This led her to confession. There she met Brother Arnaldo, a relative of hers and a friar who would become her confessor and the transcriber of her revelations.

After the full confession of her sins, Angela began a five and a half year process, "making only small steps at a time," to free herself from her past and live more fully in the way of her new calling.

About 1288, early in her conversion process, all the members of her immediate household—husband, sons, and mother, whom she had seen as impediments to her spiritual growth—died. She sold her country villa, "the best land that I owned," and gave the money to the poor. By the summer of 1291, Angela had sold most of her remaining possessions and made her profession in the Third Order of St. Francis.

Accompanying Angela was a woman named Masazuola who was Angela's spiritual companion and confidante. It is likely that Masazuola started out as her servant and stayed with Angela after her conversion. Angela recognized divine graces in Masazuola, saying she was "a marvel of simplicity, purity and chastity."

Most of what we know about Angela comes from the *Memorial,* the document transcribed by Brother Arnaldo from 1292 to 1296 that chronicles her inner journey and encounters with God, and the *Instructions,* a collection of her letters and teachings.

When she died in 1309, her body was laid to rest in the church of San Francesco in Foligno. Many people from the surrounding area came to pay their respects. Soon after she was given the title "Blessed" by a those who honored her life and work.

CATHERINE OF GENOA

Catherine was born in 1447, the youngest of five children, to Giacomo Fieschi, former viceroy of Naples, and Francesca di Negro, each of whom were from wealthy families of Genoa, Italy. When Catherine was thirteen, she attempted to enter an Augustinian convent following the path of one of her older sisters, but was refused because of her age. This was a disappointment since she had already shown herself to have "a gift of prayer" and an approach to the spiritual filled with "prudence and zeal." This rejection, combined with the death of her father in the next year, led to difficult times for Catherine. Soon after their father's death, her older brother arranged a marriage for Catherine with another powerful member of Genoa society, Giuliano Adorno. The Adorno and Fieschi families were bitter enemies, so it is likely that the arrangement was made for financial and political reasons. With her marriage at age sixteen to Giuliano, Catherine entered a ten-year period of loneliness and depression. Her new husband was spending his fortune recklessly and was known to be unfaithful and have a mistress and child. She withdrew from the social life of Genoa and became even more depressed. Then, during confession in Lent of 1473, Catherine sought God's help for her emotional state. At that moment she experienced a sudden and overwhelming feeling of God's love. She was overcome with an awareness of her own sinfulness and God's mercy. From that moment Catherine's life was transformed. She began a yearlong period of penance, prayer, and working among the poor in Genoa. Giuliano, too, experienced an amazing transformation. After becoming bankrupted, the ultimate disgrace for an aristocrat, he also experienced a conversion and spent the rest of his life working alongside Catherine, caring for the poor who were sick. Countering the social conventions of the day, Catherine also sought to forgive her husband's unfaithfulness and extend care to his former mistress and child.

Several years after her conversion, Catherine became the director of the Pammatone Hospital, a large, charitable institution that served the area. Her spiritual sensitivity, intelligence, and dedication to the poor and to the rights and position of women, along with her attention to renewal in the church and social institutions, make Catherine's legacy important to us today.

CATHERINE OF SIENA

Catherine, the second youngest of twenty-five children, was born Caterina di Giacomo di Benincasa in 1347 in Siena, Italy. Catherine's family was part of the merchant class. Her father worked as a wool dyer. They lived not far from the church and cloister of San Domenico, where she became acquainted with the Dominicans. As a child she spent many hours there, visiting her foster brother who had become a Dominican.

Catherine was a unusually devout child, recalling later to one of her spiritual advisors that at age seven she promised "her virginity to God." At age fifteen Catherine resisted her parents' efforts to see that she married by defiantly cutting off her hair. At this time she also refrained from going out except to mass at San Domenico. It is likely that she taught herself to read during this time of self-imposed solitude. By the age of eighteen she had taken the Dominican habit with a group of women called the Mantellate, mostly elderly widows who lived at home and worked under the direction of the Dominican friars to serve the needs of the poor and sick in the community.

In 1368, at age twenty, Catherine had an intense spiritual experience that she described as a "mystical espousal" to Christ. As a result, she committed her life to Christ and the work of the Mantellate, serving as a nurse to the sick in homes, in hospitals, and on the streets. Even though she had had no formal education as a youth, Catherine became known for her ability to teach theology and interpret the Bible. She was sought out as a spiritual director as well as a skilled negotiator in the political affairs of the papacy. During this time she continued to have mystical experiences and practiced austere penances, abstaining almost totally from food and sleep.

In 1374 another outbreak of the plague struck Siena. Catherine urged her friend and spiritual director Raymond of Capua and others to help her in ministering to the sick and dying. Her leadership skills were extraordinary. Catherine founded a convent, worked for church reform, carried on extensive correspondence with church leaders, and preached, being greatly in demand.

When she was about thirty, she wrote a book called the *Dialogue*, a theological debate with God. It uses argument and metaphor to expertly reveal the ideas that love and truth are intimates and that humanity finds its perfection in union with God.

In the early months of 1380, a year or two after "her book" was published, Catherine fell victim to the practices of penance she had imposed on herself. After years of abstaining from food, she was finally unable to swallow food or water. She grew weaker, lost the use of her legs and was confined to bed. Two months later she died at age thirty-three.

CLARE OF ASSISI

Clare was born in 1196, the third of five children, to Ortulana and Favarone di Offreduccio, wealthy nobles in Assisi. When Clare's mother was pregnant with her, she often visited a nearby church to pray. After praying for the safe delivery of her child, Clare's mother reported hearing a voice say, "Do not be afraid, for you will joyfully bring forth a clear light that will illumine the world." When the baby was born, her parents named her Chiara or Clare, which means "clear or bright one."

By the time Clare was fifteen, her parents had chosen a husband for her. But Clare, who had grown to be quite beautiful, resisted this plan. She had heard the preaching of a youthful and enthusiastic monk named Francis of Assisi and was moved by his message. She arranged a meeting with Francis in secret and received his advice "to despise the world" and be wedded to Christ, preserving "the pearl of her virginal purity for that blessed Spouse Whom Love made man." Clare embraced Francis's counsel and ran away from home in 1212 when she was sixteen. She then made a commitment to Francis and the other brothers to follow Christ and the way of poverty.

Clare's family tried to convince her to return, but she refused. Instead she found a home at San Damiano, one of the churches that Francis restored after his conversion to God and a life of poverty. There she organized a group of women, the Poor Ladies of San Damiano, also known as the Poor Clares. They followed the way of Francis and pursued a relationship of unwavering devotion to God through spiritual discipline and service. In her letters and other writings, Clare advocated for a life of prayer that focused one's attention solely on Christ, and yet would move the follower into everyday life. She exhorted, "Gaze upon Christ, consider Christ, contemplate Christ, as you desire to imitate him."

In the *Testament,* Clare expressed the teachings of Francis concerning poverty: to live "without anything of one's own." This demand was even more significant for Clare and her cloistered community since they were not free to beg for alms like the monks. Instead they relied on the generosity of others and a faith in God's providential care to provide for their daily needs. It is possible that Francis wanted the Poor Clares to lead a more public life, moving from place to place like the brothers, serving the poor. But the idea that women could live this way was too scandalous for the time. Church leaders in Rome ruled that Clare and the sisters should live in an enclosed community, saying that an itinerant life would create hardships too unbearable for them. This ruling points to the larger struggle they faced: being permitted the right as women to make decisions affecting the community without interference or patronization.

Clare's leadership abilities were recognized by many, including Francis. He insisted that she become abbess of the community. It was a position she lived as "servant" and "handmaiden" with the tenderness of a mother, rather than as hierarchical ruler. She encouraged the practice of discernment in the community, as elaborated upon in the *Rule,* recognizing the gift of "divine inspiration" of each of the sisters in San Damiano. She remained the abbess until her death in 1253 at the age of fifty-seven.

GERTRUDE MORE

Gertrude was born in 1606 in Essex, England, and given the name Helen. She was the daughter of the great-grandson of Sir Thomas More. When she was five her mother died, and her father, Cresacre, took on the responsibility of educating his gifted and intelligent child.

At the age of seventeen, Helen left England to enter a Benedictine convent in Cambrai, France. There were no such communities near her home since the monastic houses in England were dissolved during the Reformation. On the last day of 1623, Helen, along with eight other young women, became a Benedictine novice and took the religious name Gertrude.

The year that followed was extremely difficult for Gertrude and the others. Unsure of her calling, Gertrude was troubled by the idea of a lifelong commitment to the Benedictine community. The other novices were experiencing similar struggles. The young women wrote to the president of the English Benedictine congregation requesting help. The president responded by sending Father Augustine Baker to Cambrai to be a spiritual guide for Gertrude and the other young women. Father Baker was well suited for the task. At age forty-nine, he had already experienced the ambiguity of questioning faith and longing for God that the young women described. At first Gertrude was resistant to his guidance. But he listened well and encouraged her to pray with a "simplicity of soul . . . aided by Divine grace."

Gertrude found a new world opening to her. Her previous guides and confessors gave "no other advice than to overcome all things by force and violence," employing methods which were authoritarian. In contrast, Father Baker invited her to turn to God (not to him), to be patient with herself, and to allow God's grace to transform her. She wrote of his counsel: "For this he gave me some instructions . . . and referred me for the rest of that point to God. . . . God did make all things that were necessary for me to know so plain that I wondered to see such alteration in my soul."

By 1629 the fledgling community at Cambrai had matured enough to lead itself. Gertrude and another nun, Catherine, were nominated for abbess. Because both of them were younger than the approved age for such an appointment, the matter was referred to Rome. Catherine, who was six years older, was chosen. Gertrude was named her assistant and directed the lay sisters. The two enjoyed a fruitful and collaborative working relationship for four years. Then, in 1633, when Gertrude was twenty-seven, she became critically ill. She was admitted to the convent infirmary with a very infectious case of smallpox and died several weeks later.

Gertrude's gift to contemporary spirituality is the idea of simplicity in prayer in the midst of life. She wrote: "No employment which religious women have in religion can hinder them after they have a good entrance into prayer; because if they pray not at one time they can easily pray at another, or, best of all, pray with the work itself, and make the work their prayer."

GERTRUDE THE GREAT OF HELFTA

Gertrude was born on January 6, 1256. At the age of four she entered the monastery at Helfta near the modern city of Eisleben in eastern Germany. Little is known about her family and the circumstances surrounding her placement at the monastery at such an early age. Most young women entering monasteries at this time were required to be at least fifteen. It is possible that Gertrude's family was affected by the upheaval in Germany that eventually led to civil war and that the monastery provided a safe haven for her to grow up. Or perhaps her parents, in piety and devotion, were offering her to God. Regardless of the reasons, it is clear that Gertrude received an excellent liberal arts education there. Her education focused on Latin grammar, rhetoric and dialectic, music, geometry, arithmetic, and astronomy, as well as knowledge of the writings of the early church theologians, such as Augustine and Bernard.

In 1280, at the age of twenty-four, Gertrude had a series of spiritual experiences that led her to devote her study to theology instead of liberal arts. Even as a mystic and visionary, she continued her intellectual inquiry by teaching and writing biblical and theological commentary, prayers, spiritual exercises, and extracts from the early church fathers.

Gertrude died about 1302.

HADEWIJCH OF ANTWERP (BRABANT)

There is little information about the early life of Hadewijch. She lived in the middle of the thirteenth century and was part of a religious movement taking place in western Europe, especially in the Low Countries, that was characterized by a devotion to the purity of the Gospel message of love. She was a Beguine, a woman devoted to following the way of Christ without taking vows to be a nun. The Beguine movement offered women an alternative to the choice of marriage or the convent at an early age. As a Beguine, a woman could pursue spiritual and intellectual interests with other women and, perhaps later, choose marriage. At first Beguines lived at home, supporting themselves through manual labor such as spinning or handicrafts. Then groups formed to live, work, and pray together, under the leadership of a mistress. Hadewijch was part of such a group and became its mistress. Later her leadership was challenged for some unknown reason and she was forced to leave the community in disgrace.

From her writings we know that Hadewijch was a well-educated woman from the upper class. She was familiar with the work of the early church writers, such as Origen, Hilary of Poitiers, Augustine, Isidore of Seville, and Gregory the Great. She was completely absorbed by the theme of mystical love in her writings. In *Poems in Stanzas* she developed a new genre by employing a popular form of the day, love poetry of the court, to express her love for God. In these lyrics, God is portrayed as *mine,* "the lady," to whom she, as the suitor or *minnesanger,* longs to be near.

Along with the gift of Hadewijch's literary genius is her gift of spirituality. In her book *Visions* she tells of her mystical experiences with such intensity and seriousness that the reader is invited to enter into the experience as well. This seems to be her mission, as she indicates in Vision 8. There Christ tells her, "Lead all the unled!"

Hadewijch's teachings focus on the need for the faithful to grow in love. This message is as important today as it was for the young Beguines whom she led centuries ago.

HILDEGARD OF BINGEN

Hildegard was born in 109, in a small town not far from Mainz on the Rhine river. She came from a noble family and was the youngest of ten children. Her parents offered her, at the age of eight, to God by placing her in the care of a relative, Jutta, who lived at a Benedictine monastery. There Hildegard was educated in academics and music, showing great promise. One of the monks, Volmar, took a special interest in her and later became her secretary, confidant, and lifelong friend. At fifteen Hildegard took vows as a Benedictine nun. By this time Jutta had become the abbess of the convent associated with the monastery.

As a child Hildegard was troubled by visual disturbances, seeing people and objects glowing in brilliant light. In her first visionary work, the *Scivias* (an abbreviation of *Scito vias Domini,* "Know the ways of the Lord"), in which she used images to illustrate theological concepts, she described an episode at age three or so in which she experienced a light so bright that "my very soul shook." These visions continued throughout her life, sometimes accompanied by severe physical symptoms similar to migraines.

In 1136, Jutta died and Hildegard was elected abbess of the community. Shortly after her election, Hildegard entered into a time of extraordinary creativity. Encouraged by Volmar, she began writing the *Scivias,* composing music for use in the convent, and writing scientific works in physics and medicine. Another acclaimed mystic, Bernard of Clairvaux, took notice of her writings and recommended them to Pope Eugenius III, who became a great supporter and encouraged her to publish her work.

In her later years, Hildegard continued to take risks and challenge the establishment. In 1150, against the wishes of the abbot, Hildegard followed a vision and began a new convent independent of the monastery. Some of the sisters disagreed with the idea and did not follow, including Hildegard's beloved friend Richardis von Stade. A vision later in life also directed her to leave the sheltered life of the convent and travel around the countryside on a preaching tour, an extremely unusual occurrence for a woman of that time.

Before Hildegard died in 1179, she founded another community of nuns at Eibingen near Rudesheim.

JULIAN OF NORWICH

Julian was born in 1342. Except for her birth year, nothing else is known about her early life—birthplace, parentage, or upbringing. What is known comes from Julian's book *Revelation* (also called *Showings*), as well as an account by Margery Kempe, an eccentric mystic, of her consultation with Julian about spiritual matters.

Julian, which was likely not her birth name, took her name in honor of St. Julian at Conisford in Norwich, England, the church where she was anchoress. An anchoress was a type of spiritual advisor who vowed to remain in her cell near the church, keeping strict prayer times and occasionally meeting with those needing spiritual guidance. In addition, she might earn money by spinning or practicing another craft. Often a servant would be employed to bring food and other needed supplies to the anchorhold.

Although she called herself "unlettered" and "lewd" (ignorant), Julian was very familiar with the Bible (the Vulgate) and other religious writings, including the work of William of St.-Thierry. Her clarity of thought and theological depth come through in her work. She is known for her ideas that believers are never separated from God, even by sin, and that God is "our Mother."

Julian lived in tumultuous times. The Hundred Years' War, the Black Death, cattle disease, famine, and the Peasants' Revolt in 1369 had devastated England. In the religious world, the Great Schism (1377) and persecution of those who wrote in English instead of Latin (the Lollards) were taking place. Julian herself could have been risking persecution by writing in her own language rather than Latin.

At the age of "thirty and a half" Julian became critically ill. For three days she was near death. During this time she experienced the "Showings," a revelation of Christ's death on the cross. She wrote down the vision in *Revelation,* an intensely graphic depiction of the horrors of Christ's suffering. It climaxes with a dialogue with Christ, who assured her of God's love, saying, "You will not be overcome" (*Revelation* XXII).

The exact date of Julian's death is unknown, except that it was after 1416, when a will mentions her by name.

MARGARET EBNER

Margaret was born around 1291 in Donauworth. It is likely that members of her family were leaders in the judicial system of Donauworth since her family name, Ebner, means "arbiter, referee, judge." In 1305, when she was about fifteen, she entered a Dominican monastery, Maria Medingen, near Dillingen on the Danube as a chorister.

In 1312 Margaret was overcome by a severe and mysterious illness which caused her great suffering. The illness sometimes confined her to long periods in bed and required the constant care of another sister.

In 1332, when Margaret was mourning the loss of the sister who had cared for her during her illness, Henry of Nordlingen, a secular priest, came to visit her at the monastery. Their meeting was the beginning of a lifelong friendship. Henry, whom she called "the Friend of our Lord" in her writings, recognized Margaret's gifts and encouraged her, as her spiritual director, to record the experiences God had given her. Even though illnesses continued to plague her until her death, Margaret's spiritual life, made known in *Revelations,* was characterized by joy, consolation, peace, power, and an immense ability to express love and blessings to her immediate circle of friends and beyond.

MARGUERITE PORETE

Marguerite was born in the late 1200s in the Flemish province of Hainaut on the border of France. Not much is known about her early years, except that she became a Beguine and wrote *The Mirror of Simple Souls* sometime between 1296 and 1306. The book, written in Old French, was a guide to help believers on their spiritual journey. It took the form of a dialogue between Love, Reason, and the Soul. In it Marguerite outlined seven stages of spiritual growth through which persons move as they grow spiritually toward union with God. She also described the relationship between love and knowledge within the believer, which, as they increased, contributed positively to the goal of transformation and spiritual unity.

In 1306 *The Mirror of Simple Souls* was condemned by church leaders as a book "filled with errors and heresies." Suspicions against Beguines and their male counterparts, the Begards, had been growing among the some Franciscans and Dominicans. When the book was denounced, Marguerite was forced to watch while the authorities burned it. Then she was told not to communicate her ideas again in any form. It appears that she ignored this ruling because in 1308 she was arrested by order of the Dominican inquisitor William of Paris and jailed. During her imprisonment, the inquisitor commanded that she and her defender, Guiard de Cressonessart, swear an oath of allegiance prescribed by the inquisitor's office and request absolution— but she refused. William of Paris consulted the ecclesiastical lawyers, who judged her a heretic. Marguerite's trial took place one and a half years after she was first imprisoned. She was condemned as a relapsed heretic and burned to death on June 1, 1310.

MECHTHILD OF MAGDEBURG

Mechthild was born about 1210 near Magdeburg, a town in Saxony on the Elbe River. Little is known about her family, but it is likely that they were well-to-do. Her major work, *The Flowing Light of the Godhead,* indicates that she was a well-educated woman of the times. When Mechthild was twelve she had her first mystical experience, described in her writings as a visit from the Holy Spirit.

In 1230, when Mechthild was nearly twenty-one, she joined a community of Beguines under the direction of the Dominicans. For the next forty years Mechthild practiced the spiritual disciplines of prayer and fasting, wrote extensively, and was a voice for reform against materialism and moral indifferences in the church. Her zeal brought on the ire of the clergy and other ecclesiastical authorities, especially when she called them "liars under holy appearances" and "stinking goats." She ignored their warnings to stop writing such severe words about the abuses she observed and the leaders she accused.

But Mechthild's writings about the spiritual life were

also filled with poetic imagery, metaphors, and themes from courtly love songs. And she used biblical imagery to convey as sense of God's unconditional and compassionate love for humanity. It is clear that she was familiar with the writings of Bernard of Clairvaux, William of St.-Thierry, Hildegard of Bingen, and Gregory the Great. She was the first mystic to write in the vernacular instead of Latin and to describe a vision of the Sacred Heart of Jesus, developed later by Gertrude the Great of Helfta and made popular by Margaret Mary Alacoque in the eighteenth century.

In 1270, when Mechthild was about sixty, she sought refuge from her critics at the convent in Helfta, where Gertrude of Hackborn was abbess. The community welcomed Mechthild with gracious hospitality. Shortly after her arrival, Mechthild became seriously ill and then blind. With the help of the sisters, she was able to complete *The Flowing Light of the Godhead,* her seventh and final book, by dictating it to them. She died at Helfta between 1282 and 1284.

TERESA OF AVILA

Teresa was born on March 28, 1515, in Avila, Spain, one of ten children, to Don Alonso Sanchez de Cepeda and Doña Beatriz de Ahumada, his second wife. When Teresa was twelve her mother died. Several years later her father placed her in a school run by Augustinian nuns. It was there that she experienced the first callings to the religious life. When she expressed this desire to her father, he was not willing to let her leave. Then, in 1535, Teresa ran away from home to the Carmelite monastery in Avila. Her father finally agreed to this move, and two years later Teresa made her profession to the order. In 1538 she became seriously ill and returned home for treatment. The illness was so extreme that it left her unable to walk for three years and caused her much pain throughout the rest of her life.

In the years that followed Teresa experienced difficulty in her spiritual life. Then, in 1554, she underwent a conversion and found new strength in her call to Christ. For Teresa, this renewal led to a new manner of praying, that of passive, quiet prayer filled with visions and locutions. When challenged to explain these "supernatural" experiences of prayer, Teresa wrote *The Book of Her Life,* which is now one of the classics in Christian spirituality.

Teresa's warmth and personality attracted many people. In 1562 she started another monastery. She also wrote several important works, including *The Way of Perfection, The Book of Foundations,* and *The Interior Castle.* Her definition of prayer indicates the kind of relationship she had with God: "Mental prayer . . . is nothing else than an intimate sharing between friends; it means taking time frequently to be alone with [God] who we know loves us."

At the time of her death, in 1582, Teresa had founded fourteen monasteries. She had also traveled throughout Spain, meeting rich and poor, royalty and simple tradespeople, bishops and country priests, and helping to negotiate the affairs of the day in Spain's golden age.

Sources

Regis Armstrong, ed., *Clare of Assisi: Early Documents* (New York: Paulist Press, 1988). Copyright © 1988 by the Province of St. Mary of the Capuchin Order as represented by Rev. Regis J. Armstrong, O.F.M. Cap. Used by permission of Paulist Press.

Ellen L. Babinsky, trans., *Marguerite Porete: The Mirror of Simple Souls,* The Classics of Western Spirituality (Mahwah, N.J.: Paulist Press, 1993). Copyright © 1993 by Ellen L. Babinsky. Used by permission of Paulist Press.

Joseph L. Baird and Radd K. Ehrman, trans., *The Letters of Hildegard of Bingen* (New York: Oxford University Press, 1994). Copyright © 1994 by J. L. Baird and R. K. Ehrman. Used by permission of Oxford University Press, Inc.

Alexander Barratt, trans., *Gertrud the Great of Helfta: The Herald of God's Loving-Kindness* (Kalamazoo, Mich.: Cistercian Publications, 1991). Used by permission of Cistercian Publications.

Edmund Colledge and James Walsh, trans., *Julian of Norwich: Showings,* The Classics of Western Spirituality (New York: Paulist Press, 1978). Copyright © 1978 by the Missionary Society of St. Paul the Apostle in the State of New York. Used by permission of Paulist Press.

José De Vinck, *Revelations of Women Mystics: From Middle Ages to Modern Times* (New York: Alba House, 1985). Used by permission of Alba House.

Matthew Fox, *Illuminations of Hildegard of Bingen* (Santa Fe: Bear & Company, 1985). Used by permission of Bear & Company.

Mother Columba Hart, trans., *Hadewijch: The Complete Works,* The Classics of Western Spirituality (New York: Paulist Press, 1980). Copyright © 1980 by the Missionary Society of St. Paul the Apostle in the State of New York. Used by permission of Paulist Press.

Leonard Hindsley, trans. and ed., *Margaret Ebner: Major Works,* The Classics of Western Spirituality (Mahwah, N.J.: Paulist Press, 1993). Copyright © 1993 by Leonard P. Hindsley. Used by permission of Paulist Press.

Bruce Hozeski, trans., *Hildegard von Bingen's Mystical Visions: Translated from Scivias,* introduced by Matthew Fox (Santa Fe: Bear & Company, 1995). © 1986. Used by permission of Bear & Company.

Serge Hughes, trans., *Catherine of Genoa: Purgation and Purgatory, The Spiritual Dialogue,* The Classics of Western Spirituality (New York: Paulist Press, 1979). Copyright © 1979 by the Missionary Society of St. Paul the Apostle in the State of New York. Used by permission of Paulist Press.

Kieran Kavanaugh and Otilio Rodriguez, trans., *Teresa of Avila: The Interior Castle,* The Classics of Western Spirituality (New York: Paulist Press, 1979). Copyright © 1979 by the Washington Province of Discalced Carmelites, Inc. Used by permission of Paulist Press.

Thomas Kepler, comp., *An Anthology of Devotional Literature* (Grand Rapids, Mich.: Baker Book House, 1977). The Catherine of Genoa selection, "Sin, Purification, Illumination," originally appeared in Friedrich von Hugel, *The Mystical Elements of Religion as Studied in Saint Catherine of Genoa and Her Friends,* vol. 1 (New York: E. P. Dutton, 1923).

Paul Lachance, trans., *Angela of Foligno: Complete Works,* The Classics of Western Spirituality (Mahwah, N.J.: Paulist Press, 1993). Copyright © 1993 by Paul Lachance. Used by permission of Paulist Press.

Suzanne Noffke, trans., *Catherine of Siena: The Dialogue,* The Classics of Western Spirituality (New York: Paulist Press, 1980). Copyright © 1980 by the Missionary Society of St. Paul the Apostle in the State of New York. Used by permission of Paulist Press.

E. Allison Peers, trans. and ed., *The Life of Teresa of Jesus: The Autobiography of Teresa of Avila* (New York: Image Books/Doubleday, 1991). Used by permission of Sheed & Ward, 115 E. Armour Blvd., Kansas City MO 64141 (1-800-333-7373).

162

 Gabriele Uhlein, *Meditations with Hildegard of Bingen* (Santa Fe: Bear & Company, 1983). Used by permission of Bear & Company.

Margaret Winkworth, trans. and ed., *Gertrude of Helfta: The Herald of Divine Love,* The Classics of Western Spirituality (Mahwah, N.J.: Paulist Press, 1993). Copyright © 1993 by Margaret Winkworth. Used by permission of Paulist Press.

Emilie Zum Brunn and Georgette Epiney-Burgard, *Women Mystics in Medieval Europe* (New York: Paragon House, 1989). Used by permission of Paragon House.

In addition to the books listed above, the following books were used as sources of biographical information about the mystics:

Monica Furlong, *Visions and Longings: Medieval Women Mystics* (Boston: Shambhala, 1996).

Miriam Schmitt and Linda Kulzer, eds., *Medieval Women Monastics: Wisdom's Wellsprings* (Collegeville, Minn.: The Liturgical Press, 1996).